Live. Laugh.
Love.

Coleen Nolan

Live. Laugh. Love.

CONSTABLE

CONSTABLE

First published in Great Britain in 2021 by Constable

1 3 5 7 9 10 8 6 4 2

Copyright © Coleen Nolan, 2021

The moral right of the authors has been asserted.

A CIP catalogue record for this book
is available from the British Library.

ISBN: 978-1-40871-598-7 (hardback)
ISBN: 978-1-40871-607-6 (trade paperback)

Typeset in Baskerville MT by Hewer Text UK Ltd, Edinburgh
Printed and bound in Great Britain by Clays Ltd, Elcograf, S.p.A.

Papers used by Constable are from well-managed
forests and other responsible sources.

Constable
An imprint of
Little, Brown Book Group
Carmelite House
50 Victoria Embankment
London EC4Y 0DZ

An Hachette UK Company
www.hachette.co.uk

www.littlebrown.co.uk

Contents

Introduction

When I was asked if I'd be interested in writing a guide to life, I almost spat my tea out! I said, 'You mean me? The woman with the two failed marriages who's made more mistakes than she's had hot dinners?'

'Exactly,' said the publishers. 'That's the whole point!'

As I took another sip of tea, I thought to myself, Actually, it might be quite fun to write something like that. I've been the agony aunt at the *Daily Mirror* for over ten years and I've been around the block a few times. Not in *that* way! I mean, in general.

I've also been appearing on *Loose Women* since the show first began back in 1999 (my God, is it that long?) and it's fair to say that, when it comes to discussing my private life on the show, I haven't exactly been backwards about coming forwards! It's got me into so much trouble over the years, I can't tell you. And with so many people! I just can't help myself, sometimes.

'OK, then,' I said to them. 'But as long as we can keep it lighthearted. I'm not doing anything too serious. That's the last thing anyone needs at the moment.'

Live. Laugh. Love.

Coleen Nolan sharing her experiences about life and love and offering a few words of advice is one thing, but not Coleen Nolan telling people how to live their lives. That's quite another thing. I'd spend the rest of my life in court, being sued!

'OK, then,' they said. 'You're on.'

Six months on and here we are. A book by me – *not* telling people how to live their lives!

I always knew I wanted this to read like a conversation. As though me and you, the reader, were sitting down with a cuppa, having a chat. Granted, it'll be a bit of a one-sided chat, but you know what I mean. It seems more natural. If you want to swap the cuppa for a glass of wine, go ahead. I've had to stick to tea while I've been writing, as wine makes my face starts to puff up like a football, and rum and coke – my occasional tipple – well, we'd probably end up with a colouring book! I'm such a cheap date.

The subjects I've covered in the book are basically the ones I get asked about the most; at the *Daily Mirror*, on *Loose Women* or when I meet people face to face. There are some obvious ones in there, such as love and marriage – and divorce! – but I've also included a couple of surprises too. Well, they do say that life's full of them.

The main point of the book, though, is for us all to have bit of a laugh. God knows we need one after the year or two we've all had. And if you also manage to find a useful bit of advice along the way – thanks to my numerous mistakes and cock-ups – all the better!

Introduction

Anyway, go and get the kettle on – or the bottle opened – and let's get started.

I really hope you enjoy it.

Lots of love,
Coleen X

The good, the bad and the ugly

(Also known as love and marriage!)

I think we could all write at least one book about love, don't you? What I'm going to do is split it into three sections: 'Being Single', 'Marriage' and 'Divorce'. I'm not starting with being single though. No way. I'm saving the best till last! What I'm going to do is start off with divorce – which will be a laugh a minute – move on to marriage – which will at least have a bit of romance and a couple of good parties in it – and finish off with being single, which is the situation I find myself in at the moment.

Right, here goes!

Divorce

I'm going to surprise you and start off with a statistic, if that's OK. Did you know that, in the UK, 33 per cent of all marriages end up in divorce? I have to admit I was quite shocked when I read that. It sounds like a lot, doesn't it? It's even higher in America – about 50 per cent – so, we're actually doing OK here.

In my mum and dad's era, the rate would have been much lower; leaving the family home was unthinkable, especially for a woman, and those who were brave enough to do it were often ostracised by their families and friends. How my mum and dad stayed together I'll never know, as they didn't even sleep in the same room, let alone the same bed. At least, as far as I can remember. Maybe not sharing the same room was their secret?

When I was growing up, my family consisted of eight children and two adults, all living in a three-and-a-half bedroom house with one bathroom! My two brothers used to have to go to the pub down the road if they wanted a wash: with seven women in the house they would otherwise have to wait a very long time for the bathroom.

Live. Laugh. Love.

We obviously live in an age now where you can get divorced more easily – a bit too easily some might argue – and you have choices. When I got married, I never once thought, Oh well, if it doesn't work out, I can get divorced. First or second time! Both marriages were for ever as far as I was concerned and, despite what ended up happening, when I walked down the aisle I believed that one hundred per cent.

I was chief bridesmaid for a friend and I remember her saying to me, on her wedding day – this was just as we were walking into the church, by the way – 'If it doesn't work out I can always divorce him.' Honestly, you could have knocked me down with a feather! I remember thinking, Well, this isn't going to work. They were divorced a year later. I think what happened is that she just got wrapped up in the whole thing – the ceremony and the idea of being married – without considering what it actually meant; what it all entailed. That side of things can be quite alluring sometimes, especially to women.

I know it sounds ridiculous, me saying that both my marriages were for life but, equally, I would never have wanted to live in my mum's era when you couldn't walk away. If you're not happy in a marriage you should have the right to leave and I just happen to have exercised that right twice! But as thankful as I am that it's not frowned upon any more, walking away is often easier said than done. I get so many letters at the *Mirror* from people in unhappy marriages. It breaks my heart. One woman wrote to say she had been married for thirty years and she'd been unhappy for most of it – almost since day one. I won't go into any details for obvious reasons, but she had become pregnant quite quickly and, from then on, she said it had just felt impossible to leave.

The phrase I'm most used to reading in these kind of letters is, 'The longer it goes on, the harder it is to leave.' I don't think it's ever too late to leave a loveless marriage and the message I always try and get over to people – men and women – is that your happiness should always come above what other people might think.

Somebody said to me recently during a discussion of the subject, 'But you've had two failed marriages, Coleen.'

'No, I haven't,' I said quickly. 'I've had two really success-ful marriages.' This person looked at me like I was stupid, but I was telling the truth. Or, should I say, that's my truth. I said, 'As well as giving me three wonderful children – not to mention two ex-husbands who I'm still close to and who no longer piss me off anywhere near as much as they used to – my marriages gave me some of the happiest times of my life.'

I think this person was expecting me to focus on the shit times, but that's not the way my brain works. Sure, there were plenty of bad times, but what purpose would it serve to dwell on them? The ex-hubbies and me are still friends, the majority of the memories I have from both marriages are good ones and, between the three of us, we've brought three amazing human beings into the world. That's what I like to concentrate on and I don't care what anybody says; in my eyes, my marriages were a success.

Don't get me wrong, if I hadn't remained on good terms with Shane and Ray, I might have a different view on things, but even then only slightly. I'd still have the memories and, most importantly, I'd still have the kids. Or, should I say, adults? Yes, I should actually. One of them's thirty-two!

I think it's such a shame when people who get divorced end up being bitter. Sometimes it's inevitable, I suppose, but a lot of the time it's because they only concentrate on the end of the relationship. If I did that I'd spend the rest of my life being angry, upset and bitter. That's not to say that I don't still experience those emotions from time to time, of course. Let's say I'm talking to somebody about it. We'll be chatting away and a memory will come into my head about something Shane or Ray did and I'll think to myself, I can't believe he did that! What I don't do, though, is let those memories hang around. You're asking for trouble if you do. You obviously can't get rid of them, but what you can try and do is pay more attention to the good times. It's healthier. Take my word for it.

What really motivated me when it came to remaining on good terms with Shane and Ray – apart from the fact that I actually like them! – was the kids. Over the years, I've seen too many people use their kids as weapons to try and hurt each other. The first time I remember it happening was when I was married to Shane (happily, at that point). A friend of mine was in the process of getting divorced and they had a son who was about seven. One day at our house, while the boy himself was in the room, they started discussing who he would live with after the divorce! Can you believe it?

'Well, he's not living with me,' one of them said.

'Well, he's *definitely* not living with me,' said the other. I was absolutely gobsmacked. I remember thinking, You poor, poor boy.

Even after the divorce they went on arguing; about who would have him at weekends, things like that. It was just horrible. Not surprisingly, within a few months the son started developing behavioural issues and became a bit of a handful.

'I don't understand why it's happening to him,' my friend said to me.

'You are joking, aren't you?' I replied. 'He's standing in front of his mum and dad who are both saying they don't want him and you wonder why he's acting up? How do you think that computes in the mind of a seven-year-old?'

After that conversation I vowed that, if Shane and I ever split up, we would not go down that road. I mean, how can a parent knowingly do that to a child? It's beyond belief.

It's taken some effort on all our parts but, not only do me and my ex-husbands get on well together, so do the kids. They've got no choice when it comes to me as they're all still living at home! (I'll come on to that later.) The important thing is that the kids don't feel embarrassed or uncomfortable talking about their dads in front of me or even their dad's other halves. It doesn't bother me in the slightest.

Over the years, they've asked me what went wrong with the marriages and I've always been very straight with them: 'He was a bastard, so I kicked him out.'

Only joking.

My second marriage to Ray probably went on longer than it should have and one of the reasons for that was because I didn't want to believe that the same thing was happening again. He's a musician and we had a rocky patch previously, when he was playing a gig with Rick Astley that took him out of the house a lot. He wouldn't talk to me or make me feel special and it made me feel so insecure. At the time, we'd spoken about it and he promised to make more of an effort. Ultimately, it was the same thing that led to our divorce. When we were breaking up for good, I used to say to myself, 'What's happening, Col? This one was *definitely* supposed to be for keeps!'

I also felt really bad for our daughter, Ciara. Another big reason why I was trying so hard to make it work was because I was so worried about the effect her mum and dad splitting up might have on her. Funnily enough, she was the one who ended up persuading me to finish it with Ray. How mad is that? One night she said, 'I'm going to bed now, Mum, but before I go I just need to get this off my chest.' And then it all came out. Honestly, I've never known a rant like it! She must have gone on for at least half an hour. I remember lying in bed afterwards thinking, Well, that certainly told me! She was right, though, and the following day I finished it with Ray. Or, at least, I started the process.

Divorce

What had she said? She told me she loved us both but she couldn't carry on living in the way that we were. 'If you want to stay with him then get on with it – and stop moaning,' she said, 'and if you don't – leave.'

By my own admission, the atmosphere in the house had been horrible for ages and Ciara had had enough. Her rant made me realise that she was would be OK with Ray and I splitting up. In fact, she insisted on it!

I'm one of these people who will fight and fight to save a relationship – I'd done it before in my marriage to Shane – but you can only fight so long on your own. That was what ended up happening with me and Ray. He didn't feel there was a need to fight, so he didn't. Not because he didn't care, but because he thought that what was happening to us – we were basically growing apart – was just something that happened during a long marriage and he'd have been happy to carry on like that for ever. I just couldn't do that, which is why I pulled the plug – eventually!

We get on now better than we ever did. It's often the case with good friends who end up getting married and then divorced. Providing you're not at each other's throats, the original friendship survives everything else and is there for you to fall back on. That's what happened to us. We were good friends who ended up an item and, after we split, we went back to being good friends. During the height of the pandemic in 2020, we actually included Ray in our lockdown bubble as he was on his own in Leeds; he stayed over quite a bit during that time. But not in my room, I might add – there was none of that going on! I made him sleep with the dogs.

But for all my talk about fighting for your marriage and remaining friends with your ex, what if you're in an abusive relationship? You're not going to stay friends with somebody who's battered you for years, emotionally or physically and, if I was your friend, I'd make sure you didn't.

Unfortunately, I get a lot of letters at the *Mirror* from women in abusive relationships. I'm well aware of how easy it would be for me to write back saying, 'For God's sake, leave the bastard!' or, 'Hit him over the head with a frying pan when he's not looking.' That's what I want to say, but I obviously can't. I have to be mindful of the situation the woman might be in. My first advice is always to try and direct the woman to organisations that might be able to help them both in the long and short term.

The two words that seem to appear in every letter is 'scared' and 'helpless'. That's what makes them pick up a pen and paper or write an email. What saddens me the most is how alone they must feel. Not having somebody to talk to in a situation like that must be one of the most awful feelings there is. All I want to do is go round there in my car, run inside, kick the abuser where it hurts, grab whoever they've been abusing and take them somewhere safe. It's gratifying knowing that, sometimes, we might be able to help someone in that situation but not half as frustrating and upsetting as it is knowing that there are probably thousands more who'll never dare to seek help. I'm not an expert in anything, really, but I'm a good listener and sometimes that's all you need.

My own mum was in that very same situation and she'd never have asked for help. Great when he was sober, Dad was a horrible, horrible drunk and, although we all used to bear the brunt of his behaviour, my mum would get the lion's share. When I asked her, years later, why she never left my dad she said, 'Where would I have gone with eight children?'

I remember saying, 'Good point, Mum!'

Had she had the bravery to leave my dad, she went on, she'd have been the one who would have been blamed. 'You just didn't do it in those days, Coleen,' she said. 'Regardless of what was happening. It was just unthinkable.'

It was upsetting for us all and witnessing that abuse made me promise myself that, if I was ever in that situation, I would not hang around. I never have been, thank God. My advice to anyone who is in an abusive relationship is to try and find someone you can talk to, someone you trust who might see things more objectively. The chances are that your self-esteem will be at an all-time low and you may well have convinced yourself that it's your fault or that you're at least partly to blame. What you really need in that situation is a reality check. The realisation that you're not to blame can empower you do something positive and get out. It's easier said than done, of course, but there are a lot of organisations and charities out there who can help you through it and, although you might feel alone, you're not. Step one, then, is to reach out and get some help.

I wouldn't try to excuse the actions of my own dad, but the fact of the matter is that, the majority of the time, he was great company and the bulk of my memories of him are good ones. Like so many people though, booze was his undoing and, when he'd had too much, he turned into another person. It was classic Jekyll and Hyde. That's another thing I've done as a result of his behaviour. I'm not a drinker. As I said at the start of the book, wine turns me into a human football and the only drink I can stomach really is a rum and coke. I much prefer a cigarette to be honest – which I am castigated for on a daily basis! That said, have you ever seen anybody lose their temper, become obnoxious or be violent because they've had one Silk Cut too many? I thought not.

My dad died before my mum and, when he was on his death bed, the only person he asked for or wanted to see – and I mean the *only* person – was Mum. 'Where's Maureen?' he said constantly. 'I want Maureen.' The rest of us may as well have been invisible. Once again, I'm not trying to excuse his behaviour, but he did love her. And us. There's no doubt about that. He just wasn't very good at showing it. If you are with someone like that, who has problems with alcohol or drugs, then do everything you can to get them to seek help.

Whose idea was it to start a lighthearted book with a big chapter on divorce? Do you know, I have a horrible feeling it was me. I might have to open a bottle of Captain Morgan at this rate. Anyway, I'll try and lighten the mood a bit.

Something I thought about when writing this chapter was which one of my divorces was the hardest. Look at me, eh? Lightening the mood! Bloody hell. No divorce is easy, obviously and, by the time Ray and I got divorced, I was a very different person to the one who'd divorced Shane.

My divorce from Shane was bizarre, really, as we always got on so well. While he treated me terribly at times towards the end, we had got together and got married for a reason – because we loved each other and had a lot of fun. I like to focus on that when looking back. At the root of it all, we've always got on really well. Even when things were bad between us we'd still end up making each other laugh – and, sometimes, in the strangest of circumstances. Every time we went to court during the divorce we'd end up going for a coffee afterwards. Our solicitors used to look at each other and shake their heads. 'These two are mental!' 'What the heck are they doing?'

The only downside to this was that Shane took ages to sign the papers.

'Have you signed those papers from the solicitor?' I used to say to him.

'Shut up!' he'd reply. 'As if you're going to divorce me!' I can hear him saying it now as clear as day.

We'd always been such great mates, you see, that having to be serious with each other about such a depressing subject was difficult. The temptation was always just to laugh everything off and, had I not eventually forced myself to be hard on him, we'd probably still be married! He'd have said, 'I'll tell you what, Col, let's not bother getting divorced, shall we? We'll go for a coffee instead.'

There was no arguing with Shane, or me, for that matter. We were very determined. It took ages doing it our way, but that was better than being quick and confrontational. Come to think of it, both my divorces took longer than they should. A lot longer. At least I'm consistent!

I had ended up divorcing Shane because of his affairs. He was like a *Crossroads* heart-throb! There was one affair, in particular, that lasted a long time – about two years – and one day I just thought to myself, Come on, Col, you don't deserve that. In retrospect, I had been in denial about this one for a very long time; he'd told me the affair was over several times only to carry on with it.

If you're in this position, maybe you'll start to notice people close to you trying to point out that perhaps your marriage isn't working any more or you don't seem happy. It's hard to hear – but these people know you best and it is worth trying to see what they're saying. Maybe you will realise what you need to do much earlier.

God, I remember the moment when the decree absolute finally came through in 2003, almost four years after we'd actually separated! This'll make you laugh. Shane and I were having a cup of tea and a chat at my place about how Shane Jr and Jake were getting on when, all of a sudden, the post arrived.

Divorce

'Oh,' I said, opening the decree absolute. 'It looks like we're officially divorced now.'

'Really?' replied Shane nonchalantly. 'Anyway. What were you saying about Jake?'

It was as if I'd told him that somebody's dog had just crapped in the front garden!

My divorce from Ray was a lot harder. There was a lot of fear on his part and he didn't want it to happen. He really dug his heels in. Age was a factor. Shane and I were both in our thirties when we got divorced – it was hard but we did have time on our side, even if we hadn't appreciated it at the time. But Ray was in his sixties and he really struggled. He was also quite old-school and believed that whatever happened in a marriage, you just stuck at it. Like my mum, I suppose.

I also don't think he believed I'd actually do it, which was probably one of the main reasons it took so long. I had to convince him – coach him, even – to believe that, A, it was the right thing to do, and B, that he still had a future.

I think I was to blame, too, in a way. I had complained that I didn't feel loved quite a few times over the years – that was my main problem with Ray – and I said that we shouldn't be together any more. However, instead of following through with my threats, I always ended up convincing myself that everything would be OK and that meant we'd just go back to how it was before; same old problems.

We were both in denial, I suppose. Him because he feared for the future and was terrified of change and me because, at heart, I'm a peacemaker. When I did at last start getting serious I think Ray just believed that I was having another rant day.

Ray had also been concerned about me being the main breadwinner in our household, although it was never an issue in my eyes – as I said, he's a bit old-school. To make matters worse, he's also a Yorkshireman! You know what they say, you can take the boy out of Yorkshire but you can't take Yorkshire out of the boy. I had to convince him that I wasn't going to just throw him out on the street while he sorted himself out. Which he has, by the way. He's back in Leeds now, which is where he's originally from, and when we're not talking about Ciara or how each other are doing, he's trying to convince me that it's the best place on God's Earth. 'Best fish and chips in the world, Col,' he says.

We had mediation for a while, which really helped. When we first went, we were still living together – Ray hadn't found a house and, because of our situation, we travelled separately. After the second meeting, we travelled together and after the third meeting we went for lunch together! Once he'd accepted it was happening and that he'd be OK, he was finally able to talk about it. It was such a relief! I'd recommend mediation to anyone going through a divorce. It helped us no end and, once Ray knew that he wasn't going to be abandoned, he was fine. Or, at least, better than he had been.

He didn't half piss me off sometimes though. There is nothing more infuriating than trying to get divorced from an old-fashioned and very stubborn Yorkshireman. I remember saying to him one day, 'Why don't you want to get divorced Ray? It's the right thing to do. You know it is.'

'I can't be arsed,' he said, shrugging his shoulders.

I thought, You old charmer, you! Needless to say, the discussion went downhill from there and, as I walked away, I might have whispered one or two naughty words under my breath. I could have throttled him!

My favourite memory of Ray and me splitting up (I know, it sounds a bit weird!) is the two of us traipsing around Tesco with a trolley each, trying to kit out his new flat. Talk about useless! Every time I put something in the trolley he'd say, 'What do I need that for?'

'It's a kettle, Ray. You'll need a kettle!' It was like shopping with a teenager. In fact, it was probably worse. We only ended up doing it together because he'd already attempted to do the first shop for his new flat and had literally come back with only bread, tea and milk. 'How are you going to toast the bread, Ray?' I asked. 'And how are you going to make a cup of tea?'

He actually said something along the lines of, 'I'll just eat bread and have a glass of milk.' See what I mean by stubborn? If 'being stubborn' was a sport he'd be a world beater. In fact, my ex-husband is the Roger Federer of stubbornness!

As we walked around Tesco, pushing our trolleys, he kept looking at me saying, 'You're flipping mental, you!'

'I'm mental?' I said. 'I'm not the one who thinks kitting out a new flat involves buying tea bags, milk and a loaf of bread!' By the time we got to the checkout both trollies were full to overflowing, including a duvet, a kettle, a toaster, pillows, bedding, towels and toiletries. You name it, we had it.

I think Ray was flabbergasted by the amount of stuff we had to buy and, although he had taken the mickey out of me to start with, by the time we started unpacking it all in his flat I could see that he was starting to join the dots. You can almost hear the cogs whirring when a bloke's working something out. Bless them!

I'm so glad that Ray and I had got to a position where we were able to do that together. Not least because if we hadn't have been, he'd most probably have died of malnutrition! The thought of him having to cope with that on his own, or of Ciara not being comfortable talking about him in my presence, is almost too much to bear. It really is. I know some divorced parents who get really pissed off when the children go and spend a weekend with their ex. A friend of mine in that situation once said to me, 'They wouldn't go if they knew what he was really like.' Yet hers hadn't been an abusive relationship. They just didn't get on. My chin almost hit the floor when she said it. I remember thinking, That's right, whatever's best for the children! In all seriousness, my number one piece of advice to anyone getting divorced is always put the children first – that's something you'll never regret.

Regardless of what Shane and Ray think of me (I think they still like me, but you never know!), they idolise their kids, so why on earth would I try and tarnish that? It's just not fair. Holding on to so much bitterness is also bad for your physical and mental health.

When both my marriages were coming to an end, I was constantly tired. I remember it all too well. Part of that was down to not being able to talk about it at first, which was very difficult for me. The press would have had a field day so, for everyone's sake – but especially the kids – we kept it under wraps. I'm not saying it was easy, though. I remember appearing on *Loose Women* on a day when Ray and I were splitting up and one of the topics was what makes a marriage work. I remember sitting in the meeting before the show and, when the topic was first mentioned, my stomach just lurched. God knows how, but I managed to keep things together.

Not long after that I just had to come clean – at least to the people on the show. It was killing me inside. Me and Ray were still a long way off wanting to go public and everyone was sworn to secrecy. It was such a weight off my shoulders and, as you'd expect from a bunch of people like the crew of *Loose Women*, everyone was fantastic. Love and marriage, as a topic of conversation, I was still finding difficult and I asked if we could steer away from it when I was on the show. I said, 'I'll talk about sex, plastic surgery or stretch marks, but please, not marriage!'

What scared me most about having to take part in a conversation about marriage wasn't actually the thought of breaking down in front of everyone. I was used to that! It wasn't even the press finding out to be honest. It was the thought of having to lie to the viewers.

Live. Laugh. Love.

The only thing I'm worse at than arguing – and I'm beyond rubbish, by the way – is lying. Some people can do it at the drop of a hat but I just can't, I'm afraid. I'm not trying to make out that I'm Little Miss Perfect or anything but, for some reason, it's just not in my makeup. For me to go on live television and pretend that Ray and I were God's gift to happily married couples when we were actually in the process of getting a divorce was never going to happen in a million years. Even if I had done that, the viewers would have seen straight through it immediately. In fact, long before I made the official announcement that Ray and I were splitting up, I started getting emails and messages from viewers saying things like, 'There's definitely something up with you, Coleen. Something's on your mind.'

The same thing had happened a few years previously when Ray and I went through a rough patch: the viewers of *Loose Women* are so perceptive and, because I've always worn my heart on my sleeve on the show, they probably know me as well as many of my friends do. In fact, the viewers of *Loose Women* are like friends, really, and I mean that. When I'm down they notice straight away, offer support, and they're always rooting for me. They also know what makes me tick, which must be scary for them!

If you're a viewer of *Loose Women* and you fall into that category, first of all I'd like to apologise for being a mouthy pain in the bum sometimes but, more importantly, I'd like to say, 'Thanks,' if that's OK. I received six letters in one day from viewers and all of them said exactly the same thing. 'You're not talking about Ray as much as you used to. What's wrong?' I think one of them even referred to him as 'chicken legs', which is what I used to call him on the show. 'Old chicken legs has been annoying me again,' I'd say, while having a bit of a moan. The moment I stopped talking about Ray, the letters started coming. I couldn't do that. It doesn't matter how often I watch a show, I would never be that observant.

The biggest reaction I've ever received on *Loose Women*, at least to something I've done rather than said, was when I stopped wearing my wedding ring while I was still married to Ray. The letters and messages flooded in but, ironically, it had nothing whatever to do with us splitting up. In fact, at that point we were actually quite happy; I'd taken it off because I got contact dermatitis. I couldn't wear the ring ever again!

It's not everybody's cup of tea, talking about your private life in front of millions of people, but the upside is that there's literally an army of people out there you've never met before who genuinely care about you. It's a nice feeling, believe me. It's like having a second family. What can spoil it slightly is the press or, at least, the way they report things like a separation or a divorce. In order to sell newspapers or advertising they'll often sensationalise the story and their chosen angle may either work for or against you. It's the luck of the draw really, or perhaps it will be down to whether the editor's had a good night's sleep and is in a good mood!

I understand why they have to do it but, unfortunately, the press don't always get it factually right. Even more unfortunately, a lot of people reading the stories take them as gospel. I find that fact harder to deal with than anything, really. Sometimes the press will just change the punctuation of a quote ever so slightly and, by doing so, they'll turn the tone of the article on its head. It's clever, I'll give them that! I'm not daft, though. I know it's part and parcel of living in the public eye, but that doesn't stop it being frustrating.

When Ray and I were ready to go public about our divorce, we decided that it was better coming from me, as I'd be able to control the story that way. I'd also be able to insist that I had a say over the way the story was reported – 'copy approval', as it's called – in certain cases and, although we knew that the news would probably result in a load of follow-up stories that could be based on nothing but rumours, at least we knew that the initial one – the announcement, so to speak – would be our words and ours alone.

One thing you can't get copy approval on is a headline. The story itself might be quite boring but the headline will have to make people want to read on and the papers obviously have to be creative. Mine and Ray's announcement was basically that we were getting a divorce but were remaining good friends. A story like that might be good news to the people concerned – and it was to us – but to a newspaper editor it's the equivalent of putting a clapped-out, three-wheel van on the forecourt of a car showroom. Good news just doesn't sell newspapers, unfortunately, and if they want to run a story, a bit of poetic licence usually comes into play. I think one of the headlines read, COLEEN NOLAN IN DIVORCE SHOCKER! Well, I suppose some people might have been a bit shocked and, at the end of the day, we were getting divorced. As I said, the papers can be quite clever sometimes.

But some papers and magazines take 'poetic licence' too far. Take one magazine, for instance. I actually have a really good relationship with them, but if you were to believe everything they printed, you'd think Ray and I were about to get divorced every week from the moment we married! It was incredible. They knew things about us that even we didn't know – a *lot* of things! I used to ring them up and say, 'I've just popped out to get some milk and apparently I'm moving out! Could you tell me when, please, so I know when to pack my bag!' I remember one week seeing a headline that said Ray and I were splitting up. The story inside was that Ray was going away on tour for a month. The magazine's argument would have been that we were splitting up, just as the headline said, but only for a month – which it didn't say.

Even my family used to ring me up at least once a week and say, 'Oh, my God, are you and Ray splitting up?'

I'd say, 'You've just read that, haven't you?'

I take it on the chin these days. Somebody once said to me that you can't agree to a nice, big double-page spread when you're happily married and then expect them to leave you alone when you're not. It comes with the territory. The more truthful you are when you do speak with them, the more chance you'll have of not getting hurt.

Even though divorcing Ray was the right thing to do, reading about it in the newspapers was actually quite hard. Not because it felt like an intrusion. It didn't. Don't forget, I'd announced it! No, the thing is, it just brought every-thing home, I suppose, not least the fact that we hadn't managed to make our marriage work. There's something very final about seeing it in black-and-white. The differ-ence between the divorce from Ray and the divorce from Shane – apart from the fact that I was a lot older and more resilient when I was with Ray – was the fact that the whole process of splitting up was a lot more protracted with him. By the time we did the deed I was no longer in love. This all made it a lot easier to move on. I should have it as a skill on my CV, really: 'Getting over divorces'!

People I know who are married but have never been divorced often ask me what it feels like when it's all over. They always assume I'm going to say something like 'sad', 'lonely' or 'bereft' but, in both cases, I've felt nothing but relief and elation! Not because I was glad to get rid of either Shane or Ray. That had already happened by the time the decree absolutes arrived. It was because the process itself was at an end and I was absolutely fed up with it.

My solicitors were great, but you can only pay £150 for an email or £50 for a text so many times before it starts to rankle. In fact, I moaned about this in one of my other books so it must have got to me! That was all actually Ray's fault. Yes, it was, chicken legs! He went into denial mode after I started divorce proceedings and, for a while, he refused to engage. Every time my solicitors tried to contact him – and failed – they'd send me an email telling me what had happened. I would be charged on each occasion. I could have killed him! In the end, I had to have a word with Ray on behalf of my solicitors who were acting on behalf of me! I should have charged them, shouldn't I? I'm not blaming the solicitors, though. That's the way they make their money. All the same, by the end of it I never wanted to see another legal face for as long as I lived. They were representing me and had my best interests at heart and they wanted me to fight Ray for a better deal but, as well as costing me more money in legal fees, not to mention more time, going on would have finished me off mentally.

'Just go away, will you?' I said, as politely as I could. 'I'm fine with what we've agreed!'

It's not for me to advise anybody how to negotiate a divorce settlement but what I will say is that you should always take into consideration the effect that it's having on your physical and mental health, as well as on the health of those around you. If a solicitor or a friend or family member is telling you to hold out for a better settlement, make sure you consider every aspect and always keep in mind your health and wellbeing. Nothing's more impor-tant in that situation.

To me, the saddest thing about the process of getting a divorce – and I experienced this more after divorcing Ray – is the feeling that, after however many years of marriage, all that really matters and all anyone's really bothered about is who owns what. I found that so, so hard. Our whole marriage, everything we've been through, came down to who gets which car and who owns the house. I know it's all necessary but it cheapens everything.

When I first saw the settlement written down in black-and-white, I wanted to ring up the solicitor and say, 'Our marriage was so much more than that! Don't you people realise?' They'd have locked me away, most probably. That's how I felt though. It was gutting seeing what was once a very happy relationship reduced to what was basically a long list of belongings.

I think guilt also had a lot to do with how difficult I found my divorces. On both occasions I was the one who instigated proceedings and, regardless of whether my reasons were justified or not – and I believe they were – I was left feeling, if not exactly like I was the bad guy, then like the person who pressed the 'destruct' button. You remember what my mum said about her getting the blame if she'd walked out on my dad, regardless of his behaviour? That's kind of how I felt when I set the wheels in motion, except neither Shane or Ray were in any way abusive and the only one apportioning any blame was actually me. I was in being 'my own worst enemy' territory.

I read the other day that you can get a divorce online these days. Makes sense! You can get everything else on the internet. Why not a divorce? It's only about four hundred pounds. Not that I'd be able to do it. I bought a laptop about a year ago, after having been nagged by my kids – 'You'll wonder how you ever managed without one,

Mum,' they said – and within a week I'd given it to Jake. 'Take that bloody thing away,' I said. 'I hate it!'

I heard a rumour a while ago that Gary Lineker was one of the first celebrities to use an online divorce. I had to ask somebody to check that this was true or not – check online, obviously – so that I didn't end up getting sued, and it is. He claimed that lawyers stir up hatred to bump up their fees and so him and his – now ex – wife Danielle decided to stick two fingers up at them all by using the online system.

I did actually look into getting an online divorce from Ray but you have to be in total agreement about every-thing and, unfortunately, we weren't. You also have to be pretty switched on legally, I think, so that was a bit of a non-starter. It's cheaper than a weekend away though!

To anyone going through a separation – providing there's no abuse – I'd encourage you to leave the lawyers out of it for as long as humanly possible and talk. You cannot overstate the importance of communication in these situations and, even if it doesn't work out, you'll have arrived at that decision *because* you've communicated and hopefully you'll be able to move on.

I've got to try and end this bit on a high, haven't I really?

Despite the sad circumstances, I really did feel relief and freedom after both my divorces. Those feelings alone allowed me to start developing my sense of self-worth which, towards the end of the processes, had all but disap-peared. Feeling my confidence starting to come back again was so empowering. I didn't turn into a raging narcissist or anything; I just started feeling slightly better than useless, which I hadn't done for ages, and it made such a big difference.

One thing I would definitely recommend, if you feel like you need it, is therapy. I know it's not always associated with things like divorce but believe me, it can be a godsend sometimes. I found it really, really useful during my divorce from Shane. In fact, had I not had it, by the end I'd have been a complete and utter mess! Not only had Shane been cheating on me for a while but he refused to admit it, even accusing me of being paranoid when I tried to confront him and, little by little, his behaviour had chipped away at my self-esteem.

There were two reasons I found therapy so helpful. First, just talking about something as complicated and emotionally draining as a divorce is essential, in my opinion, and it's especially helpful to talk with somebody who's impartial. The other helpful thing was the amount of logic they used when we talked. Again, always being impartial. When your emotions are being pulled from pillar to post, your sense of logic tends to go out of the window and, just like self-worth, feeling it coming back was such a relief. I genuinely thought I was going mad during my divorce from Shane, what with all the press coverage and everybody having their opinion about what I should and shouldn't do.

Seriously, if your marriage is in trouble and your other half won't go to couples therapy – which should be the first port of call if you're at a stalemate – one-to-one therapy is the next best thing. If I'd been able to persuade Ray to go to couples therapy when things were really bad, there would have been every chance we'd still be together. I know that's quite a bold claim, but it's the truth. He would never have considered any kind of therapy though, for the simple reason that he can't open up. Ring any bells about your own partner? It will for some of you.

My sisters used to tell me off for not talking to them when I was divorcing Shane and Ray, but they were too close. 'If they're hurting me,' I said. 'You'll hate them, and I don't want that.' That said, there were times during both divorces when I would have a good old whinge to either a girlfriend or one of my sisters and that was fine – as long as it was just every so often, though.

Some people found it strange that I had started seeing a therapist. 'But they're a stranger,' they'd say.

'Exactly!' I replied. 'That's the point!'

My therapist had no idea about the two of us in my marriage and they were never conflicted or judgemental. All they were able to do was offer me common sense and that all-important logic about the realities of the situation. For example, I remember trying to persuade this therapist that Shane and I were actually best friends, despite us getting a divorce.

'Really?' said the therapist. 'If one of your girlfriends treated you the way Shane has, would they still be your "best friend"?'

'No, of course not,' I replied.

'Then why are you trying to claim that you and Shane are best friends when he's treating you so badly? Your best friend doesn't hurt you and your best friend doesn't cheat on you.' The advice was logical – that was what I needed. I carried on fighting Shane's corner for a while but, every time I did so, the therapist put me straight. 'You're deluded,' she said. 'He's not your best friend.'

Each time this happened I'd go home and think, Actually, they might be right about this. I was obviously trying to cling on to anything positive that was left of our relationship and it was doing me more harm than good. Yet, a friend or relative would never have been able to make me see the light. Never in a million years. It had to be somebody impartial.

The therapist also corrected me when I suggested, stupidly, that perhaps I should just put up with Shane's behaviour for the sake of the kids. 'OK, then,' said the therapist, 'so you want to bring two boys up in a house where they will grow up to believe that if you're a man you can basically go out and sleep with who you want because your partner will always forgive you? And if their partners complain, they'll just say, "Well, Dad did it and Mum didn't mind." '

That was one of the last things the therapist ever said to me – after that, it all made sense, and I was done. I didn't need to continue with therapy because I knew what I had to do.

Therapy doesn't only help in divorce. It doesn't matter what the problem is, at the end of every letter I reply to at the *Mirror*, I'll always advise someone to seek counselling, whether it be to help with drugs, alcohol, infidelity or abuse.

Divorce

Somebody asked me the other day if I'd ever been to a divorce party. 'No, I have not!' I said. It seemed a bit weird to me. I suppose if you've come out of a really bad relationship and people have supported you, you might want to raise a glass with them when it's all over and thank them for helping you through it. But a party? Each to their own, I suppose. Personally, I'm not really proud of the fact that neither of my marriages worked and the thought of celebrating that fact makes me feel a bit uncomfortable.

Ray and I do have what you might call 'mini-celebrations' of our split sometimes. They're very quick. Let's say he's come round to mine and, if he does something stupid or annoying I'll say, 'Oh my God, I'm *so* glad we're divorced!' He always follows it up with, 'Yeah, so am I!' and then we'll then have a bit of a giggle. Voila! There's our mini divorce celebration.

Right, I really have had enough of divorce now. Literally! Haven't you? Remember though, if you are going through one, please try and talk to somebody impartial, if you get the chance. Whether it be as a couple or you on your own. It really will help you see the wood for the trees.

Marriage

It might seem a bit strange, doing love backwards; going from divorce to marriage, but now we've been through the depressing part we can start to have some fun. At least that's what I'm aiming for. Once I get going, things might change.

I was quite young when I married Shane and his proposal would have put Rudolph Valentino to shame. It was pure romance! We were living near Uxbridge, London at the time, which already sounds so romantic, doesn't it? While we were out on a walk he just said, 'Shall we get engaged then, or what?'

I remember looking at him, open-mouthed. 'Yeah . . . OK,' I said. The first thing we did was go for a McDonald's – renowned for its intimate atmosphere – before finding a branch of H. Samuel and buying an engagement ring for about a hundred quid. Not exactly *Romeo and Juliet*, is it?

I'm actually taking the mickey a bit here. I was just twenty-one when we got engaged and, despite the lack of moonlight and roses, I was giddy with excitement. We both were. Ray's proposal was the absolute opposite of Shane's. It took place in front of all my family and friends and I had absolutely no idea it was going to happen. You see, men can actually surprise us sometimes. Even in a nice way!

The occasion of my engagement to Ray was my fortieth birthday party, at the De Vere hotel in Blackpool, more years ago now that I care to remember! Ray had organised the whole event and the only information he'd given me was where it was taking place and the fact that it was going to be black tie. I had no idea who was going to be there and obviously no idea what he had in mind. When I got to the hotel I was absolutely flabbergasted. There must have been about 250 people there. Over 200 people ready to celebrate me getting old! I remember Ray opening the door to the ballroom and there they all were. At that moment an orchestra started playing 'Happy Birthday'. It was just fantastic.

Later in the evening a big screen was lowered from the ceiling and they played messages from those members of my family and my friends who couldn't be there. It was just like *This Is Your Life*! The last message – or what I believed was the last – was from Ray, saying he hoped I'd had a lovely evening and hoped he'd done me proud, which he had. I expected the screen to go blank and everyone to get up for a dance. But there was one more video for me to watch. Ray got down on one knee, on the big screen, and said, 'Will you marry me?'

I instinctively put my hands over my eyes and, when I opened them, I saw Ray standing in front of me with a ring. You should have seen the reaction from the guests. Everyone went ballistic! The only people Ray had told, and I mean the *only* people, were my sons Shane and Jake. Ray got on very well with the boys but he obviously couldn't be a hundred per cent sure how they'd react and he had decided to ask their permission. Isn't that lovely? Fortunately, they were over the moon, so it was all good.

I had actually been wondering whether Ray was going to propose to me that day but he'd thrown me off the scent by not asking me first thing, when he brought me breakfast in bed. I didn't see a ring on the tray and I thought, That's it, then; maybe another day. I was convinced he was too shy to ask me at the party.

It just goes to show how much I know, doesn't it?

After his proposal, to which I obviously said, 'Yes,' the party had a great buzz. Everyone was just in the best mood ever. The thing I couldn't get my head around, though, was the fact that he'd managed to keep it a secret. I kept going up to people and saying, 'Are you sure you didn't know?'

'No!' they all replied. 'We had no idea.'

When they boys told me he'd asked them for my hand, I melted. 'Aww, did he?' I gushed. 'That's so sweet!'

Our wedding was fantastic, too. You see what I mean about remembering the good bits? I might not be married to Ray any more but nobody can ever take the memories from that party or our wedding away from me and I'll treasure them for as long as I live. Just as with the proposal, me and Ray went all out with the wedding – fancy location, big white dress, everything done properly – it couldn't have been more different to my marriage to Shane.

Shane and I ended up eloping to get married, so again, it was the opposite of what happened with marriage number two. I like to get all the bases covered if I can! We did have a big wedding planned, Shane and I, but a few weeks before it was supposed to happen he turned around and said, completely out of the blue, 'I don't think I can do this, Col.'

My immediate reaction was to panic. Oh my God, I thought. He doesn't want to marry me any more. He doesn't love me!

'No, no!' said Shane, suddenly realising what was going on in my head. 'I still want to marry you, Col. The thing is, this wedding has got nothing to do with us any more.'

He was right. The wedding had been taken over by our families and my husband-to-be had had enough of it. And so had I, to be honest. I remember my mum telling me that Donna, who'd been my best mate at school, could only come to the reception and not the ceremony.

I said, 'What do you mean, I can't *not* have Donna at the ceremony? She's one of my best friends.'

'Well,' said Mum, 'if you invite Donna, then you'll have to invite Mrs Boyle.'

'Who's Mrs Boyle?'

'You remember Mrs Boyle! We've known her for ever. She used to bounce you on her knee when you were a baby.'

'I literally have no idea who you're talking about, Mum!'

See what I mean? Shane and I weren't the first groom and bride to lose control of their wedding and I bet there've been thousands since. It doesn't make it any easier, though. In fact, I was actually quite lucky as the families had stopped even asking Shane for his opinion ages ago! No wonder he'd had enough.

We ended up cancelling the wedding and making an excuse. We didn't tell anyone we were eloping though. That was our little secret. Or quite *big* secret! As you'd imagine, the task of having to tell everyone wasn't one we were particularly looking forward to, but we were in for a nice surprise. Everyone, apart from my sister, Denise, who was a bit upset, was thrilled for us both. It was such a relief!

As a parent now, I do understand how these big events can get out of control a bit and, as annoying and intrusive as the interference can be, it's usually meant with the best of intentions. Or, at least, I think it is. There'll be some people who might disagree! My advice to anyone getting married who is suffering from an overbearing or interfering mother or mother-in-law is to buy some poison and drop it in her tea. Failing that, you could bite the bullet, sit them down and them that it's your day and not theirs. Not in a nasty way, but, otherwise, if you give up control of your wedding to an overbearing mother or mother-in-law and you don't get the day you've dreamed of, you might regret it for the rest of your life. You could also end up resenting that person for the rest of your life and that won't be nice.

Another idea is to see if there's some kind of compromise to be had. Anyone with half a brain will understand what's happening and meet you halfway and, if they don't, then get the poison out! Last on the advice list is straight-forward diplomacy – which in this case would be you, as in the bride, saying something along the lines of, 'Oh, that's a great idea. I'll bear that in mind,' and then forgetting about it! Actually, it's not really diplomacy, is it? It's bullshit!

My son Shane and his fiancee Maddy are getting married soon and I've had to bite my tongue so many times I've hardly got one left. The thing is, weddings can do very strange things to people and, despite me not being an overbearing person by nature, my son's wedding has turned me into one. Or, at least, potentially. Only I can stop me from becoming an overbearing pain in the arse and – so far – I've succeeded!

Going back to what I was saying earlier, if Shane said, 'Look, Mum, we want to do what you and Dad did and get married on our own,' of course, I'd be disappointed – but I'd try and hide it though, and I certainly wouldn't give him a hard time.

The only niggle of disappointment I had about Shane's dad and I eloping came some years later, at Bernie's wedding. I was the chief bridesmaid and, at the church, my dad said, 'Do you know, Coleen? One of my only regrets in life is not walking my baby down the aisle.' He wasn't being malicious. Anything but. That really stuck with me though particularly when, soon afterwards, he began to get ill.

As a result of what Dad said, in the end, Shane and I decided to have a blessing in a church, just so my dad could walk me down the aisle. To be honest with you, had we not had the blessing, my dad's comment would have haunted me for the rest of my life so, if truth be known, it was as much for me as it was for him.

I actually thought I'd hate eloping, but I didn't. My biggest worry was not having a beautiful, white wedding dress and a veil as I didn't think I'd feel married without them. 'You can still wear a veil, can't you,' suggested Shane.

'Yeah, I suppose I can,' I replied. And that's exactly what I did! I got myself a short veil to go with my dress, which was even shorter, and I was good to go.

Shane's proposal had been similarly low-key. I'd always had visions of him getting down on one knee, a rose between his teeth, somewhere like Paris or Venice. Not upright in flaming Uxbridge with a McDonald's around the corner! It was spontaneous, though, which I suppose is what made it special. Not to mention the fact that we were head-over-heels in love. It was who I was with that mattered, not where we were or whether he was down on one knee. At that moment in time, the only person I wanted to be with was Shane and, to be perfectly honest with you, he could probably have put a Hula Hoop on my finger in a pub car park and I'd have gushed, 'Oh, yes, please!' Listen to me, getting all gooey-eyed. And about my ex-husband! That doesn't happen very often. Thank God!

I'm often asked what my opinions are on really extravagant weddings and my answer often surprises people. Most people seem to be expecting me to slag them off but my opinion is this: if you've got the money and that's what you want, just go for it! It's not for me to say that people shouldn't spend a hundred thousand pounds on a wedding, just as it's not for me to say that they shouldn't go out and get drunk or fart on the bus! The only thing I would say, if it's going to leave you in a lot of debt, think long and hard first. To me, lumbering yourself with a bill that's going to take five or ten years to pay off is absolute madness.

You can't beat a good wedding though, don't you think? Providing there's a veil involved, of course. Otherwise, I won't go. The most impressive wedding I've ever been to is my sister Anne's, which took place in Blackpool in 1979. I remember looking out of the living room window of our terraced house on the morning of the wedding and all I could see was a sea of people. I just went, 'Wow! Look at that!' Apparently, there were over two thousand people outside the church and the police ended up having to close the surrounding roads.

When Anne arrived at the church in a horse-drawn carriage, everyone went berserk! There were so many people that the police had to escort her into the church and I remember being so, so impressed! The ceremony itself was gorgeous and not at all flash and yet what was happening outside was just bonkers. It was like a royal wedding, I suppose – Blackpool style!

So, what about making a marriage work? (Says the twice-divorced agony aunt!) Or, at least, what about keeping a marriage alive? As well as receiving letters from people whose marriages are in trouble, I also receive the odd one from people whose marriages are ticking along quite nicely. They are looking for what you might call 'preventative medicine', really – as what they're usually after is advice on keeping things fresh.

There's obviously no magic formula to making a marriage work. If there was somebody would be making an absolute fortune! The lawyers wouldn't like it though, would they? My God, no. It's probably a bit of a cliché but marriages are a work-in-progress and you only get out what you're prepared you put in. Not dropping out at the first hurdle helps, but, equally, you have to know when it's at an end. That's the situation I found myself in when it came to my marriages and, as I already said, I was a late-comer when it came to admitting defeat.

Do I think turbulent marriages can work? Of course they can, but only if both parties want them to. Making a marriage work is not an exact science and, regardless of what you hear and read about other people's experiences, you have to judge yours on its own merits. No two marriages are the same and that's the truth.

The thing that I believe is central for being happy in a marriage is feeling loved, and I think that's probably the same for a lot of women. And men, for that matter. I certainly get that impression from the letters I receive and from conversations I've had. Feeling loved is the founda-tion of a relationship. I couldn't give a monkey's about jewellery or flowers. Sure, it's always nice to receive some-thing from time to time, but if they haven't been sent by somebody who clearly loves you then they're meaningless. As soon as I don't feel that love I go into panic mode and I'll work and work to try and get it back. If I can't get retrieve the love, though, I'd rather be on my own. Or with fifteen animals and several young adults, which is my current situation. At least they love me! And all I have to do is feed them. It's sad though, isn't it? Over the past year I've had more love from my three pygmy goats than I have from a man! Welcome to my world.

Lightening the mood even more, let's talk about falling out. I won't say 'having arguments' as I don't really do them, but I can do falling out. If I really have to. Shane would often try and defuse the mood by making me laugh, which I think a lot of men try. Notice I said 'try'! I'd say to him, 'You're pissing me off, Shane. I'm going to bed.'

He'd then run to the door and shut it. 'You're not going to bed until you tell me that you love me.'

'But I don't love you!' I'd reply. 'In fact, I don't even know why I married you. You're an arsehole!'

'Well ,you can't go to bed then. Simple as that.'

This would go on for about ten or fifteen minutes and the longer it went on the more I'd laugh, and the more I'd laugh, the more he'd try and make me laugh even more.

'OK, I love you,' I'd eventually say. 'I don't like you and I still think you're an arsehole, but I do love you.'

'You can go to bed, then,' he'd say moving out of the way. 'Night!'

I'm not saying these exchanges always ended amicably, at least not immediately, but they never turned into shouting matches.

Ray would completely shut down: it was always the silent treatment. He could go four or five days, sometimes, without saying a solitary word to me. What made it worse was that it would never happen after a falling-out. Oh no. That *was* the falling-out! As a result, I never had a clue why he was being silent and, as long as he was quiet, I'd sit there racking my brains trying to figure it out. Frustrating? Just a bit!

I'd come in from doing *Loose Women* or something and say, 'Do you want a cup of tea?'

'No.'

Then I'd think, Here we go. I wonder what I've done this time? I should have moved Sherlock Holmes in as a lodger! 'Come on. What's up?' I'd say.

'Nothing.' He wouldn't even look at me.

'Oh, come on, Ray, something obviously is up. Just tell me.'

'Nothing.'

As I said, this could go on for the best part of a week sometimes and by the end of it I'd literally be tearing my hair out. 'Please just tell me what's up!' I'd plead with him.

'Nothing.'

The most frustrating part of this is that, when I did eventually find out what had driven Ray to take a vow of silence for the best part of a bloody week, it was usually something meaningless, like one of the dogs pooing on the carpet – and when I wasn't even there! But Ray didn't go silent maliciously. It was never anything serious, which in some ways made it even more frustrating. Had I rolled in after a three-day rum-and-coke binge with the girls from *Loose Women*, having been leering at a load of male strippers, then I could understand it.

Live. Laugh. Love.

Some people say to me, 'You never argue? That must be infuriating!' I suppose it might be to some people but, as soon as somebody starts screaming and shouting, I stop listening. It's that simple. I don't mind it if you raise your voice a bit – we all do that from time to time – but that's my limit. Equally, if two people are shouting at each other, nobody's listening anyway, so what's the bloody point?

My sisters always say that I'm so laidback I'm horizontal, but that's not true. I do have rows! I just have them in my head. If somebody shouts, I walk away, have the row in my head that would have taken place had I shouted back and then go back and calmly tell that person exactly what I think of them. That was what happened with Shane, who would sometimes shout. I'd walk off. It's a good system, believe me, as a few minutes later I'm over it. Simple! There were no threats, no recriminations, no insults and, best of all, no long silences!

My kids might say something different – the only time I ever scared them was when I went quiet. Their dads used to shout at them if they did something wrong, whereas I'd give them the silent treatment. When that happened, they knew they were in trouble! The difference was that I'd go quiet for a few minutes as opposed to days going by without a word. They used to say, 'Are you all right, Mum? We don't like it when you go quiet.' What used to scare them even more was me turning down a cup of tea. I have to be *really* annoyed to turn down a cup of tea and, when that happens, it's best to make yourself scarce. I'm like a silent assassin. A silent assassin who loves tea!

After a few minutes, I'd call the kids over and tell them why I was annoyed and, because they didn't like upsetting me, they'd also make an extra special effort to put things right. An extra special effort that would normally be forgotten about the following day, of course. After all, they were just kids.

Nine times out of ten these standoffs would be about tidying. Surprise, surprise! After realising that they'd incurred my wrath they'd scurry around with dusters and dishcloths trying to make amends. 'I've done the kitchen, Mum!' one of them would say.

'Have you?' I'd reply, trying not to be enthusiastic. It never lasted long. As long as they always realised what they'd done wrong and then tried to put it right, I couldn't ask for more, really. And that's exactly what they did.

One thing I haven't mentioned in relation to marriage yet – and this can happen in almost any situation, providing you're attached – is cheating. I've been cheated on. I've also been the one who's done the cheating. The first piece of advice I'd give to anybody who's been cheated on is, before you respond, for heaven's sake take some time and calm down. Then go back and kick him in the balls!

Only joking.

It might take a few hours or it might take a few days but unless you're calm, or as calm as you possibly can be, you won't be able to make any sense of anything, which will just prolong the agony. As important, being worked up will prevent you from making decisions about what to do next – whether that be finishing the relationship or trying to carry on. Equally, whoever's cheated has to be honest and open about why it's happened, otherwise you won't get anywhere.

I cheated on Shane for a while and, although I had my reasons, I regretted it. But instead of allowing it to consume us and ruin our relationship, we managed to make it bring us closer together. We definitely had to work at it but the two years that followed were probably the happiest we had together. Later, he ended up cheating on me and, because of what had happened previously, I was ready to listen. Once again, we talked everything through and, after a few weeks, things were OK again.

One thing I'm dead against in these situations is using infidelity as a stick to batter each other with. If you've decided that you're going to forgive somebody, you can't keep bringing it up in every bloody argument. You may as well say 'Goodbye,' as it'll never work in a million years. You have to move on, one way or another – it's as simple as that. I thought Shane and I had reached a situation where we had both moved on but, unfortunately, he hadn't finished the affair. Once I found out, that was that and there was no coming back from it. You do have to acknowledge when enough is enough and where to draw the line. I don't regret giving Shane a second chance but, ultimately, when I realised he had continued to lie to me, that had to be the end – I stuck to my guns and I don't regret that either.

I didn't trust him and I would worry when he went out for a newspaper. I hated feeling like that. He'd go out to work and I'd immediately start going through his pockets. I even used to check his bank statements. I was frantic; frantic and very, very paranoid. It got to the point where I couldn't wait for him to leave so I could turn into Inspector Clouseau for the day. Fortunately, it eventually dawned on me that, as well as being very bad for my mental health, the person who was doing this wasn't like me at all. Me, a paranoid obsessive? Absolutely not. That's what made me finish it with Shane in the end. Well, that and the fact that he was still having an affair, of course. The bastard!

I had a friend years ago whose husband had an affair. They had four beautiful kids and when she found out she was absolutely beside herself. They ended up having counselling together and I'm happy to report that they're still married to this day. More importantly though, they're blissfully happy together. I think that a lot of people who've cheated on somebody believe that, if the other person forgives them and decides to stay, they can both just sweep the whole thing under the carpet and pretend it never happened. They don't think they need to be respectful of their partner's feelings going forward. The reverse is true. You obviously don't want the injured party bringing it up every five minutes, but at the same time, if they have a bit of a wobble and want to talk about it, you have to be prepared to agree. Equally, I know people who just can't let it go and will carry on bringing it up time and time again.

The thing is, you can never trust anybody one hundred per cent, for the simple reason that we're all human and we can all make mistakes. It probably seems a bit cynical at first glance, but everybody is capable of making a bad choice – I don't care who you are. Unfortunately, some people are under the illusion that their relationship is completely cheat-proof. They're the ones who end up getting hurt the most. Your pride gets such a kicking if it happens after you've spent years slagging everyone who's had an affair while telling everyone how perfect your relationship is and that neither of you could ever be unfaithful. You'll have a lot further to fall. In fact, you'd probably have to go into hiding! I've known loads of people over the years who haven't believed it could happen to them and I honestly can't think of one who hasn't ended up with egg on their face.

Beware!

A question I'm often asked is whether or not things changed for me after I got married. The reason people ask is because I lived with Shane and Ray for a long time before we tied the knot and there's an assumption sometimes that putting a ring on each other's finger can actually spoil things. My answer is always the same: 'Yes, it did change things. Twice! Thanks for reminding me!' In all seriousness, there probably is an argument for not getting married if things are going well and there obviously will be some instances where doing so has spelt the end. It could just be a coincidence, of course. But is it always?

My sister Maureen and her husband were together twenty-six years before they got married. Three years after their wedding they split up! I must admit I have heard a lot of similar stories but, equally, you probably never hear about the ones that work. As I said earlier, you have to judge each situation on its own merits.

Despite living with both my husbands before the weddings, I did feel different when we got married. I can't actually describe the feeling very well, but it was lovely. It was a mixture of love, security, commitment and together-ness, I suppose. The feeling was stronger the first time around, I think. Probably because I was younger and it was all very new and exciting.

The press also treated us as couples differently after we got married. It was almost as if we hadn't been together before that, despite us even having had a child together. Then, as soon as we tied the knot – with the press very kindly reporting it to the world – we were suddenly Mr and Mrs!

I'll tell you what people don't consider when they're getting married and that's the fact that every few years people do just change. And, to be honest, why on earth would you think of that just as you're heading to your special day? Yet it's true – the person you are and the person you're with will be different – sometimes drastically – twenty or thirty years into your relationship. It's the things you share in common that can stop you faltering. You know, kids, your friends, and where you live, etc. But what about when the kids leave home? Suddenly, the fact that one – or even both of you – might have changed suddenly comes into the spotlight. Shit! you think to your-selves. We might not have anything in common any more!

I get a lot of letters along those lines and, if it isn't the kids leaving home that sets the cat among the pigeons, it's retirement. Sometimes people will throw themselves into their jobs when their kids leave home and, even if they have already grown apart from their other halves, the chances are it'll remain hidden. Or, at least, enough for neither of you to want to rock the boat. When you retire, there really is no hiding place.

If I had a pound for every letter I've received from people who've recently retired containing the words, 'I don't know if I can carry on living with them any more,' I'd be able to clear the national debt. It's such a sad situation. Imagine being with somebody for thirty years or more and then discovering, usually in a matter of weeks, that you no longer want to share your lives.

I haven't really mentioned compromise yet, but it is essential to making a marriage work. Nobody particularly likes doing it, but – unless you're in the unfortunate position in which your feelings and happiness aren't considered important – a marriage won't last five minutes without compromise.

I do think that men sometimes struggle when it comes to compromise. I don't want to sound sexist when I say that (isn't it funny that when somebody says something like, 'I don't want to sound sexist,' you know for a fact that they're about to do just that! I was just warning you, that's all) and I'm going to have to try and back this up, I suppose.

OK, why do I think that men find compromise more difficult than women? That's easy. Because they've had it their own way for so long! It's that simple, I'm afraid. If you look at marriage throughout the ages, women – as the so-called 'weaker sex' – have always been the ones who've been expected to give in. I can't blame it all on men though, as much as I'd like to. Overprotective mothers are some of the biggest culprits when it comes to allowing men to believe that it should always be their way or the highway. My God, some mothers can be infuriating! They're female chauvinist pigs, basically.

The most common example I read in letters to the *Mirror* is a man who will go out with his mates one week-end and then refuse to go out with his wife the next. 'I don't want to do that,' they say. 'It's boring.' At first, this sort of attitude is just annoying but, after a while, it starts to hit home that the person you're married to doesn't actually want to spend any time alone with you. They don't want a romantic meal out or even a cosy night in with a takeaway. That's quite a sobering thought really. Don't you think? You've made a commitment to this person – had kids with them, bought a house with them, got married to them – yet what they're doing is basically rejecting you. That must be how it feels. How could it not?

What's even worse is when a man does compromise but makes it clear he's doing it under duress. That really is demoralising. You're sitting there, trying to make conversation on a night out together, and all he's thinking about is the fact that he'd rather be down the pub with his mates and he's checking the football score on his phone under the table.

Fortunately, I still hear the odd example of couples who've made things work; compromise is usually a big part of their formula. The difference between them and the others is that, A, they actually enjoy spending time together and B, they make an effort when it comes to their plans. Marriage-by-numbers can only work for so long in my opinion – or, at least, it can only make you happy for so long. Going for a meal at the same restaurant once a month, just because you think you should, isn't going to make either of you happy. As I said earlier, you have to work at every aspect of a marriage and compromise is no different. It's about figuring out what will make your other half happy and what makes them tick. I'm not saying I was God's gift to marriage or anything, but nothing made me happier than surprising Shane or Ray and knowing that in turn I'd made them happy. Equally, when they did it to me, the result was the same. It has to be give and take, every time.

While I've been writing this I've been trying to think of couples I know who appear to have nailed the whole marriage thing and the first one that springs to mind is my niece and her husband. When I say 'nailed it', who knows what will happen in the future? At the moment, though, they're very much the real deal.

Compromise is obviously at the heart of their relation-ship and, despite them having kids, they haven't forgotten that they're a couple as well. That has to be one of the hardest things to achieve, as having kids can be so all-consuming. But my niece and her husband are always going away together for a night or two and they have more date nights than a randy teenager! How much effort that takes them I have absolutely no idea but it's definitely paying off. No marriage is perfect, but theirs is as close as I've ever seen. You watch, now I've said that – in five years' time, my niece will be down the pub with her mates getting sozzled on prosecco and he'll be at home sobbing into a Mills & Boon!

Sometimes my niece and her other half come to ours for a party and when they do, they'll check into a Premier Inn nearby and make a weekend of it. By seven o'clock the kids will be knackered but instead of plonking them on a sofa and carrying on drinking they'll just take them back to the hotel and have an early one. The thing is, both of them are drinkers and they promise to come back on their own the following weekend and stay up all night! That, too, is a form of compromise and, what's more, it works. For them, that is. It might not work for others. If they ever split up I think I'll give up on marriage all together! All hope will have disappeared if that happens.

My daughter, Ciara, who's twenty in June, lives here with her boyfriend and they're the same as a couple in many ways. She's had boyfriends in the past who I've taken one look at and gone, 'This'll last two months,' and it has. With this boyfriend, though, it's different and I actually look at them sometimes and think, You two could genuinely be together for the rest of your lives.

Yes, I know I'm a hopeless romantic but having been married twice before – and having made one or two mistakes along the way – I get a feeling about what might work and what won't and these two work, believe me. What makes their relationship even more fascinating is the fact that they're both so young. It's fascinating and heartening. I'll stare at them in absolute wonder sometimes and I'll think, How can two people this age get it so, so right? The answer is they both give and take, they both listen to each other and they make time for each other. They've been together about eighteen months now and I don't think I've ever seen them row. That'll probably change! Who knows, in Ciara's eyes, perhaps she's learned from my mistakes? She certainly doesn't take any shit from him. She'll go, 'It's your turn to tidy the bedroom and wash the sheets.'

I would never have said anything to Shane or Ray about housework like that. I'd have just gone and done it. I know it sounds miniscule but in the grand scheme of things – as in, laying the foundations for a long-term relationship – something like that can be absolutely massive. If I hadn't washed the sheets during either of my marriages those sheets would still not be washed! I'd get the odd comment like, 'These sheets are a bit smelly?' but that'd be it. They wouldn't actually do anything about it. As opposed to actually saying to either of them, 'Look here, you. Get those sheets cleaned now, otherwise you'll be for the high jump!' I'd just do it myself and have that conversation in the head. I must have imagined thousands of scenarios over the years of me berating Shane and Ray for not pulling their weight. Actually, it's probably more like millions!

Marriage

They always ended with me storming off and them saying 'Sorry.' Ha! As if that would ever happen.

I'm pretty sure Ciara must have noticed that happening, though (me doing all the work, not talking to myself!) and when she finds herself in that situation she reacts. To be fair, her boyfriend, Max, is a lovely lad and I don't think she's had a great deal of practice of having to talk to him about such things, at least, not so far. I'll come down in the morning sometimes and he'll have cleaned up or emptied the dishwasher. Then he'll come in and say, 'I'm going to the shops. Do you want anything?' I sit there thinking, What planet are you actually from?

My sons and their girlfriends – who I love, by the way – all take the mickey out of me. 'You're always going on about Ciara and Max,' they moan. 'They're your favourites.' I'll just sit there looking at my nice clean kitchen and empty dishwasher and say, 'Yes, they bloody well are!'

The thing we all need to take away from this chapter isn't the fact that 33 per cent of all marriages end in divorce. It's the fact that 67 per cent of all marriages *don't*! I don't think that's a bad figure really, bearing in mind how easy it is to get divorced these days, not to mention how easy it is to mess around, if you see what I mean – don't you worry, I know all about Tinder! I also know how many of the people on there are married! Well, I don't have an exact figure, as such, but from my experience – which is pretty vast now, having been single for a while – there's more than one or two! Anyway, I'll be coming on to all that shortly.

Live. Laugh. Love.

I do believe in the institution of marriage and, despite my own experiences, I think I always will. Millions upon millions of people still want to make a commitment to each other beyond just sharing a house and having kids and I for one think that's amazing. And who knows, if more of these people make more of an effort to make each other feel loved and enjoy each other's company, perhaps we can get the 33 per cent figure down a bit? Who knows? Just carry on concentrating on the positives. I should be a marriage counsellor really, shouldn't I? Coleen's Counselling Ltd.

If I was a counsellor, though, and I had to give advice to a man who was having problems, one of the first things I'd say to him – this is after I'd told him to wash his own bloody underwear occasionally and put the lid down on the toilet – is that when it comes to a happy marriage it's the little things that matter. Little and often. Forget the grand gestures. Make your wife a cup of tea in the morning sometimes or just put a wash on. As well as making her life easier, it helps to maintain the attachment you had when you got married and reminds you that you're both in this together. That's the one thing I never got from either of my marriages and I know it would have made a big, big difference. Oh, to have been made a cup of tea first thing in the morning! I'm a simple girl with simple tastes and I make no excuses for it.

Being single

I did say that I was going to leave the best till last, didn't I?
Well, here we are. Being single! I've talked a lot over the
years about what it's like being married, especially on *Loose
Women*, but being single is still a bit of a novelty. I'm not
sure whether it's an age thing or just because I've been
married a couple of times but, God, am I enjoying it! It's
so, so different to what I've been used to, but in a good
way.

Being single after divorcing Shane was terrifying. There
was nothing good about it at that point. I was in my mid-
thirties and, because I had two young kids, I thought
nobody else would want me. I also felt like a bit of a failure
because my marriage was over; my self-esteem was at rock
bottom.

You'd think that being in the same situation in my early
fifties, which was where I was when Ray and I got divorced,
would have been even harder in some respects: I'd been in
relationships almost constantly since I was fifteen years of
age. What's more, they'd all been long relationships. My
first lasted from the age of fifteen to nineteen, then I was
in another one from nineteen to twenty one, then I met

Shane, who I was with until 1999, then I saw a new guy for nine months and then I met Ray. The point being that, since the age of fifteen – so, a good thirty-five years or so, well over half my life – I'd never really had any time alone – you know, any time for me.

I'm not saying that I regret any of the relationships I just mentioned, but you probably know what I mean. Being single is similar to being in a relationship though, in that you can only appreciate what it's like once you experience it. I wasn't sure how I'd feel once Ray moved out, although I wasn't nervous. I was looking forward to it, really, for once not having to think about somebody else all the time; somebody else's feelings, movements and opinions. You know what it's like. What's that old saying? 'Familiarity breeds contempt.' I wasn't just divorcing Ray. I was divorcing the idea of being in a long-term relationship. Or, at least, I was asking for a lengthy separation!

What I think helped me get to that position was becoming self-sufficient. When I was with Shane, he was the bread-winner and, after we split up, I still relied on him for a time. At least financially. It's not very liberating, believe me. With Ray, it was the other way around and I was the major earner. When we got divorced, it was the first time in God knows how many years that I was able to make decisions by myself without having to consult anyone else. Now that *was* liberating!

I obviously still had the kids but if they didn't agree with me, tough! My house, my rules. Get used to it! Even moving into a new home, which can be one of the most stressful things you can do in life, especially after splitting up with somebody, was just amazing. Everything was on my shoulders – finding the right place, making sure the kids were happy, arranging the removal people, swapping the mortgage. I even enjoyed sorting out the sodding bills! It was all my responsibility and mine alone. And it all went according to plan. There were no tears, no arguments with utility companies, no angry phone calls to removal men. Everything went as it was supposed to and, without wanting to blow my own trumpet – although I'm going to – it was all down to me. Men? Who needs 'em!

Best of all, when it came to choosing a new place to live, I was able to make sure that it was going to be big enough to accommodate my animals. I'd been wanting to get more for years and figured that this was the perfect time. I've always had dogs before but never more than two, and I wanted more than two! I also wanted cats . . . and goats . . . and elephants!

Both Shane and Ray had kyboshed the idea of having more animals around the place before. It was always, 'I'm allergic to cats' or, 'Two dogs are more than enough, Col! I don't want another one.' Because I'm a bit of a softy and because I believed in compromise, I'd always given in. Now though, the only person I had to give in to was me! The result is I've now got four dogs, six cats and three pygmy goats. I'm like Dr Doolittle! Not least because I talk to them all, whether they want me to or not.

Another thing that makes the single life easier is the kids still being at home, particularly because I've got such a great relationship with them. Would I be as mad about being single if they weren't around? I certainly wouldn't be as happy as I am, but I'd definitely still love being single. I've never actually experienced being completely on my own before, at least not for a prolonged period, and I couldn't actually tell you how it would affect me. When the kids often go off and do their own thing for a week or two, I am always absolutely fine. I am glad when they come home, though. I always am, even after a few hours. The kids were obviously around a lot more during the lockdown in the pandemic, but then we all had to stay at home at that time.

Do you know what annoys me a bit? The fact that so many people assume that just because I've got a history of being in long-term relationships, I must be itching to find myself a man and move in with him. It's a fair enough assumption, really, as I obviously have form. But it's not fair that they think I can only really function at all if I have a man and am in a steady relationship. Let me tell you ladies, *nothing* could be further from the truth!

Would I like to have some fun if the right man came along? You bet I would! Would I be against it going further if it felt right? Possibly. Never say never, that's my motto. I'm not exactly over the hill! Or, at least, I don't think I am.

What's changed with me is what I want from a relationship. With Shane and Ray it was the traditional marriage thing, whereas now it's more about companionship. I don't mean 'companionship' as in somebody who watches telly with me occasionally and escorts me to the supermarket. As I said, I'm not that far gone! I'm also not ready to give up on romance yet. It's hard to when you're a hopeless romantic like me!

What I mean is I'm looking for somebody who is maybe more of a friend. A 'friend with benefits', I think they call it. Yes, that's what I want. A friend with benefits! One thing I'm not ready to do – and won't be for a very long time I'd imagine, if ever – is surrender my freedom. I'm happy at the moment. Happier than I've ever been, quite possibly. As a state of mind, it's extremely addictive. I've been content before, but it was within what I suppose they call a nuclear family – you know, two parents and a couple of kids. Being content on your own is a different thing all together, and mainly because it comes with a massive dollop of freedom!

By the way, I have had a couple of relationships since splitting up with Ray. The biggest difference with my earlier, longer experiences of being in a couple was the fact that I did so because I wanted to and not because I felt I needed to. Does that make sense? There was no yearning to be loved or to have a happy-ever-after.

Don't get me wrong, I did *want* to have my relationships with Shane and Ray. I married them, for heaven's sake! Each time I was definitely in serial-monogamist mode; I felt a yearning to actually be with somebody. That yearning has now gone, thank God, which has allowed me to look at men in a different way. I don't *need* a man any more, that's the new thing. I might want a man occasionally, if you know what I mean. You know, for a chat and a trip to a museum. But I don't need to be with one. It can all be on my terms now, and for the first time ever.

What I'm very grateful for is having not turned into a man-hater. I've seen that happen on so many occasions (sometimes with good reason) and it's never nice to watch. If I was harbouring any kind of bitterness towards either of my marriages I wouldn't be as happy as I am now. Just the thought of being that way makes me feel physically sick. I don't hate men. On the contrary, I quite like them sometimes. Especially when I can switch them off! Or, in my case, swipe left.

I think I've already mentioned Tinder, haven't I? I've definitely talked about it on *Loose Women* once or twice. Some people seem to think it's funny that a woman in her mid-fifties is prepared to use an app in that way, but why not? I can swipe left or right with the best of them! Talking of which – and this is no word of a lie – last night I swiped left about two thousand times on Tinder. Honestly, I'm not joking! I actually got cramp in my finger by the end. How depressing is that, though? I thought to myself, I'm not doing this again.

No disrespect to the men I swiped but I know my type and not one of them fitted the bill. Perhaps I'm getting choosier in my old age? Or should I say, more discerning? Most of my sisters are on Tinder so, although we're not singing together any more, at least we're all on the pull! What do you reckon? I'm in the mood for dating . . . actually, we've just finished filming a follow-up series to

Being single

The Nolans Go Cruising and *At Home with the Nolans*, in which they try and set us up with men. I bet you can't wait, can you?

The first man the TV crew tried to set me up with was not my type at all – that's putting it mildly – and when they first showed me his photo, I'm afraid I laughed for a full ten minutes! I said, 'Please don't show that! It'll demoralise him!' The thing is, as opposed to asking us what kind of men we actually liked, they just picked them themselves. Perhaps that was the idea, to leave things more to chance? Well, if it was, it certainly bloody worked! They also had to pick people who would be willing to go on telly, which must have narrowed it down a bit. Honestly, I was an absolute flaming wreck when they showed me this photo.

It all started off with another photo for my sister Linda. I looked at it over her shoulder and said, completely tongue-in-cheek, 'Ooh, he's nice, Lin. You're in there!'

'Get stuffed, Col!' she said, laughing.

'Aww, come on,' I said. 'He might be lovely!'

After having a good giggle about her potential match they brought in mine and that's when the fun started. It wasn't just me, by the way. The crew were crying with laughter, to the point where the camera was actually shaking! I was quite insulted that they thought this bloke would be my type and, had I not been wetting myself for ten or fifteen minutes, I'd probably have given them a bollocking. Linda ended up going on a date with somebody that we, the sisters, picked for her and, although she didn't fancy him, he was a really nice guy.

Live. Laugh. Love.

I think I enjoy flirting as much as I do dating, which makes Ciara sick. I feel young, though, and it's obviously less complicated! I did actually speak to a man online for a few months recently and we ended up going on a couple of dates. This was before lockdown and, as the first date got closer, I became more and more hesitant. By the time the day arrived I was in a right state. I actually felt (and acted!) like a fourteen-year-old again, although I only real-ised that afterwards. It suddenly struck me that this is how I used to feel all those years ago and I was able to have a laugh about it.

I actually really liked this bloke and we were due to start dating again after lockdown. But he phoned and told me, 'I can't deal with who you are. It's not going to work.' So that was that. I'm hoping he meant it was my fame he couldn't deal with, such as it is, as opposed to my character or personality! Either way, I did think to myself, Hang on, it's taken you six months to come to that conclusion? Thanks very much!

That night I was back on Tinder, having a few swipes, so it was OK. Plenty more fish in the sea, as they say! Actually, that's the name of one of the websites. Not that I'm giving them a plug or anything; Tinder's definitely my favourite at the moment. At first I thought it was just a shagging app, but somebody put me right. 'It can be,' they said, 'but it doesn't have to be.'

The whole process of being on Tinder does sound like a bit of a cattle market –that swiping left or right thing – but, at the end of the day, it's no different to going on the pull in a nightclub, is it? If somebody asks you if you want a drink or a dance in a club or at a bar, you know what their intentions are and you either say, 'Yes' or 'No.' On Tinder, the selection process is quicker, left or right, and it's a lot cheaper! It's not nearly as much fun though. Then again, a woman in her mid-fifties going on the pull in a nightclub – or being pulled for that matter – isn't a good look really.

You do get a lot of married men on Tinder, not surprisingly, and a lot of them are quite open about it. The two excuses they usually give for having a profile on the app are the old favourites, 'My wife doesn't understand me,' and, 'My wife doesn't want to have sex any more and has agreed that I can come on here and try my luck.'

I wouldn't be interested in that, but even if I was, I'd be asking for proof of that interesting statement. 'Can I speak to your wife about that, please?' I'd ask. 'I'd just like her to confirm that she's OK with me jumping into bed with you.' You wouldn't see him for dust!

You obviously have to be very careful on these apps because, at the end of the day, you have no idea who you're talking to. Marcus from Manchester who is forty-one, good looking, and drives a Porsche, could actually turn out to be Dirty Derek from Doncaster who's seventy-one and has a wig and two whippets!

As with all of these things, I think you have to wade through an awful lot of crap to get to anyone nice (hence my two thousand left swipes the other night!) and you *always* have to be on your guard. That's about all the advice

I can offer really. Avoid the Dirty Dereks and the weirdos if you possibly can and always meet in a very public place!

At first, I fought against the whole online thing as, to me, it just seemed bizarre. I thought, This is nothing but a bloody catalogue! Then it started to dawn on me that, actually, it's not too bad. Getting picked up in a nightclub or a bar would be a bit grubby by comparison, especially at my age. Actually, it'd probably be impossible! You know what I mean, though. I think even younger people would these days be less inclined to go home with somebody they've literally just met in a bar than they would have been twenty or thirty years ago. I mean, why on earth would you, if you can go online and try before you buy? Sure, I get the whole spontaneity thing and I too have been in a situation where I've met somebody and thought, Yes, please! You have to be so, so careful though, and especially these days.

A problem I have is that I sometimes don't know if somebody's showing an interest in me because I'm famous or because they actually fancy me. Apart from having my wits about me there's nothing I can really do so, unfortunately, I just have to go with the flow and hope for the best. If they are only talking to me because I'm famous it'll usually show after time. I know pretty much straight away because all they want to know is what the girls are like on *Loose Women*, or what it was like being married to Shane.

There was that man I mentioned earlier who didn't want to be with me because I'm famous. I found that frustrating, but I kind of had to respect it. He's quite a private person and that's fair enough. What was annoying was the time it took him to reach that conclusion. I did warn him right at the beginning that my world could be a bit mad sometimes (understatement of the year!) but at first he said he was fine with it. Bloody men, eh?

Something I get asked about a lot at the *Mirror* is age gaps. To me, it's just a question of degree, really, and what I usually suggest is that people consider what their relationship might be like in later life. If a woman of forty-five, for instance, starts dating a sixty-year-old you probably wouldn't bat an eyelid. Not these days! Providing you both remain healthy you'll always be close enough in years for it not to seem too strange.

Let's now add a bit more time to that and imagine a forty-year-old who's dating a seventy-year-old. I appreciate that seventy is supposed to be the new fifty (which would make me thirty-six!), but in twenty years' time that seventy-year-old is going to be ninety and the partner will only be sixty. I know quite a few sixty-year-olds who are full of life and might feel burdened by a ninety-year-old partner. You're always going to get the odd one that works, of course, and that's great. I would never advise anybody not to start dating somebody they liked because of an age gap. Within reason.

The rule for me, personally, is that I would never date somebody that I could have given birth to. That rule could obviously vary a bit, but you get my drift. The guy I just mentioned was eight years younger than me. The thing is, eight years is nothing these days and had he been eight years older I wouldn't have batted an eyelid either. I remember thinking, Oh, my God, he's in his forties and I'm in my mid-fifties!

Look at Carol McGiffin from *Loose Women*, though. Her husband's about twenty-two years younger than she is and it doesn't bother them in the slightest. Once again, it's not an exact science; there will always be exceptions to every rule. Carol might be older in years than her husband but she's still more of a party animal. They also don't have kids, which makes a difference. But, for me, to go out with a thirty-six-year-old when I have a son who's thirty-two would just be too weird. It would be the same if Shane Jr came home and said that he was dating a women of fifty-six. I'd be like, 'WHAAAAAT?!'

One thing I will not tolerate are singletons in their fifties – or even their sixties and seventies, for that matter – saying that they're past it and are too old to date. If I was in my twenties, I'd probably agree with them as, at that age, you genuinely do believe that people over forty shouldn't even hold hands, let alone go out on dates or have some fun between the sheets. Now I'm in my fifties, I realise what a load of rubbish that is. We might not have the energy of our younger friends and we might be a different shape, but what we lack in that department we more than make up for with experience. Not just in *that* department! I mean in life experience.

A woman wrote to me a while ago who was in her seventies to say she'd been having a great time online. And offline, I think! Fortunately, the people who run dating sites have cottoned onto the fact that older fiddles are still capable of playing good tunes and there are almost as many websites for older people as there are younger ones. Mind you, what constitutes younger these days? It all depends on who you speak to, I suppose.

My advice to anybody who has recently become single and wants to get back on the horse would be to go for it and do not be swayed by your age. As I said, there are websites out there now that cater for every age group. What you have to do, though, is manage your expectations. You get a lot of weirdos and timewasters on these sites and apps. Take it from somebody who knows! In that respect, though, it's no different to being in a club or a bar, really. Come on, we've all been chatted up by weirdos in nightclubs, haven't we? In general, apps and websites are a lot safer (as long as you follow the appropriate precautions when it comes to meeting someone in person), so just take the weirdos and timewasters in your stride and ignore them. And be patient! That is an absolute must if you're going online. If you think you're going to find the 'one' in a day or two you're probably going to be disappointed.

Apart from that, my other main piece of advice would be not to rush things. If you meet somebody you like online it's very tempting to say yes to a meeting straight away (well, if you're not in lockdown!), but please don't rush into anything. And, if you do meet, make sure it's in a *very* public place!

Another reason people are a bit nonplussed about me being on Tinder is they assume that I meet a lot of eligible people at work. Why would she need to go online? they wonder. But most of the people I work with are either eighteen, gay – or both – and the ones that aren't eighteen or gay are all married. There's nothing there for me, take my word for it! I see lots of very beautiful people at work but they're just kids. If I worked on *Countdown* I might be in with more of a chance but I wouldn't know an anagram from an angiogram!

I think the best thing about online dating for me so far is how much it's helped me through lockdown. It's safe and you can flirt as much as you like from the comfort of your own home. And sometimes with people you fancy! For a lazy home-bird like me that's a dream come true. It has done more than allow me to flirt, too. I've had some great chats with people I'm not interested in romantically and I've made some good friends. OK, so they're virtual friends, but so what? They make me laugh sometimes and, as I said at the start of the book, we all need a few of those at the moment.

One thing I will say though is that, in order to enjoy your time online – and this goes for dating in general – you have to learn to be comfortable with your own company first and that means learning to love yourself. That's so, so important. If you don't have that self-respect you'll just end up with the wrong person again, as you'll go with the first man who offers you love and company, and that could be anyone. The reason I give this advice is because that it's exactly what I had to do before I started dating again. My self-esteem had taken a bit of a battering and before I started swiping (left, mainly!) and flirting I had to sort it out.

Unlike after Shane, following my divorce from Ray I didn't have therapy. The decline had lasted so long and, at the risk of repeating myself, I was ready to start living again and the only therapy I needed was that. Seriously, just enjoy the freedom, learn to love yourself, and then find out what you *really* want from life. Who knows, after that you might decide that you're not ready to start dating. Never say never though.

Just enjoy this moment and make life about you!

You can choose your friends, thank God!

You can concentrate on friendship more when you're single. I certainly have and, although I was never discouraged from seeing my friends when I was with Shane or Ray, the fact is that, without them, I've got a lot more time on my hands.

My first best friend was Linda. She was three years older than me and was the person responsible for getting me into horses. She wasn't rich or anything. None of the people I knew when I was young were rich. She had this little pony and I used to go with her down to the stables after school. Although I probably didn't know the true meaning of friendship at such a young age – we became friends when I was about five or six – Linda and I were inseparable. When my family and I moved to London when I was nine I remember being very upset. You always mean to keep in touch in that situation, but the truth is that children tend to move on quite quickly, once the initial sadness has subsided, and it was no different with me and Linda.

Funnily enough, one of my other best friends when I was growing up in Blackpool was a boy called Alan whose family lived next door and Linda was, and still is, best friends with Alan's sister. I'm not sure why Alan and I got on so well but we were at that innocent age when you'd have conversations about getting married when you're older. Alan is married now, but not to me. The cheating bastard!

I never ended up keeping any friends from my child-hood, partly because I moved to London and partly because I always had one eye on what I was doing after school with the family; I regret that in a way, but then what can you do? By the age of fifteen I was touring the world with my sisters and the truth is that, after moving to London, I never really had time for friends. This isn't a sob story, by the way. I was just more reliant on my family at that age but I've more than made up for it since then.

I think my oldest friends – as in the ones I've been friends with the longest – are Carol, Jane and Vickie. I met them when Shane Jr joined the local football team when he was five. For some reason, the three of us just clicked and, when things started going bad with Shane Sr, they saw me through everything. Especially Carol. She still lives in London and although I now live in Cheshire and we don't see or speak to each other very often, if she knocked on my door now, it'd be like I only saw her yester-day. Also, she's always the first person I'll think of if I'm organising a party. I think we all have friends like that, don't we? It just goes to prove that, when it comes to people who you're genuinely close to, out of sight does not mean out of mind.

You can choose your friends, thank God!

Because of the industry I'm in and because I'm quite sociable, I probably know hundreds of people in total. The thing is, if I left the job tomorrow, I'd probably only keep in touch with four or five of them. Not because I don't like the others, but because they're more like acquaintances than friends and, in my experience, it's difficult to have such an intense relationship – the kind you have with a close friend – with more than a handful of people. I couldn't be close friends with fifteen or twenty people. I wouldn't have time to breathe!

I used to do summer seasons with my sisters and each year we'd spend months and months with the same group of people. The same dancers, musicians and stagehands. It was like being part of a family and when it all came to an end it could be gut-wrenching. But when it comes to making and keeping friends, working in showbusiness is a bit like being a child really, in that if you're ever parted from a colleague you promise to keep in touch, but will soon become distracted by whatever you're doing next. It's the nature of the beast. And as with kids, the sadness only lasted until we'd started working with a new crowd of people. So, unlike my friend Carol, for instance, it would actually be a case of out of sight, out of mind. Not because showbusiness folk are shallow, but because relationships like ours are usually of their time and remaining close with everyone you work with just isn't possible.

One of the strangest experiences I've had when it comes to best friends happened just a few years ago and is a mystery to this day. I became friends with a woman via the stables which house my horses and we quickly became close. The relationship itself was based around laughter as much as anything else and we were in and out of each other's houses every day. She was so full of life, this woman, and that's despite the fact that she'd had a really hard time of it, what with one thing and another. She never moaned, though, and always managed to retain her glass-is-half-full outlook.

Then, out of the blue one day, after about two years of being what I would still describe as best friends, she stopped talking to me and stopped being my friend. There was no warning and no reason. She just stopped talking to me – literally, overnight.

The only potential catalyst for her not speaking to me was her falling out with the woman who owned the stables where our horses lived. The thing is, though, not only did that have nothing whatsoever to do with me, but this woman ended up moving her horse to different stables around the corner. It just didn't make any sense.

By the way, when I mention stables and horses, you probably think I'm talking about elegant thoroughbreds and posh women from the Cheshire set wearing millions of pounds of plastic surgery and ultra-expensive jodhpurs. Wrong! Just because you have a horse doesn't necessarily mean you have money, and the kind of stables I'm used to are usually full of old nags that have been rescued from dog-food factories. And that's just the women! Given a choice, I'd always go for the latter look as I refuse to have plastic surgery, won't spend more than twenty quid on a pair of jodhpurs and prefer my horses to be old and a bit slow, like me!

I'd become so close to this woman and we had spent so much time together; all my other friends were as puzzled as I was. Why had she dumped me? Nobody's ever been able to get to the bottom of it. Even now, about three years on, it's still brought up in conversation sometimes and we're all still completely nonplussed. It'd be all right if we'd had a row or something – well, not all right, but you know what I mean. I'd at least have a reason.

I genuinely thought that she was going to be a lifelong friend and it affected me for about six months. Not just the fact that we weren't friends any more, but the manner in which it happened. I didn't cry myself to sleep every night, but it played on my mind a lot. It was like an itch I couldn't scratch! Eventually, I phoned her and asked her what had happened.

'Oh, nothing,' she said quite nonchalantly. 'I've just moved yard.'

I said, 'I didn't think that when you moved yard you had to move friends too. You've only moved across the road!'

'No, no,' she said. 'I just need to sort the pony out and then I'll be round.'

I haven't seen her since. She's still in the area; friends of mine have seen her, but not me.

One thing you can't do in situations like this is allow the problem to get under your skin. That's easier said than done, of course, and because it's such a mystery I've found it difficult sometimes. I want to know everything! You've also got to make sure that it doesn't affect your other relationships going forward. I always say that I'll trust anybody until they let me down – tarring everyone with the same brush just perpetuates everything and makes you miserable.

The question people often ask me when I tell them this story is, 'What would you do if you ever saw her in the street?' Well, I'd speak to her and be civil, and I'm ninety-nine per cent sure that she'd do the same. I would never let it become a friendship again though. Too much water has passed under the bridge and it would always be the proverbial elephant in the room.

I was with Ray when this woman and I first became friends and, for some reason, he never liked her. Everybody else I knew loved her and, as I said, we were like a couple of twins. I used to think that Ray was just jealous because I'd met somebody who I enjoyed spending a lot of time with, but in hindsight perhaps I was wrong. The first time she ever came round to the house he said he didn't like her. He waited until she'd left, of course, but as soon as she had he turned to me and said, 'I don't like her, Coleen. I don't trust her.'

'Piss off,' I replied jokingly. 'She's lovely!' Looking back, perhaps he knew something I didn't.

At the end of the day, I think friendships are just like relationships, in that you can easily grow out of each other or grow apart. I'm not suggesting that that's what happened in this situation, but I've had friends in my past who, when I've seen them again years later, have turned into acquaintances – or ex-friends, if you want to put it more bluntly.

You can choose your friends, thank God!

We just don't have anything in common any more. As with a relationship, you also have to learn to let go sometimes and there have been instances in my own life where I've worried about the fact that I'm not as close to somebody as I used to be. It can happen for a number of reasons and the trick is to try not to overanalyse it. These things happen!

Instead of worrying about the ones that get away, look after the people you're still close to and enjoy being their friend! I've got three girlfriends coming round this Saturday for a girlie night in and there aren't many things I look forward to more, to be honest. It'll no doubt get a bit rowdy and there's a definite chance that at least one of us will end up having a bit too much to drink – although it won't be me, of course! What better way to spend a Saturday evening, though, than in the company of three of your best friends? You certainly won't get that with acquaintances. Always remember, it's better to have one really good friend than a thousand acquaintances.

The friend of mine who's least like me is probably Ruth Langford. We're like chalk and cheese in so many ways, yet I just adore her. For a start, she's very well-spoken and educated whereas I speak with a northern accent and I left school at fifteen. Her lifestyle is very different to mine, as are many of her attitudes, yet when we're together we just click. I love having a friend who isn't an obvious match. I don't speak to her every day and we've never been to each other's houses, but somehow it works. If I had to give a reason I'd say that it's probably because we're both honest;

what you see is exactly what you get. Also, if I think Ruth's being a dick about something I'll tell her, and vice versa.

I have been able to find a few positives when it comes to friendships and social media, which may come as a bit of a surprise – you'll hear me go on about social media a bit later but it's safe to say that I'm not always a fan. Yet it can be useful when it comes to friendships. I sort of wish it had been around when I moved to London aged nine or when I was on tour with my sisters; I'd have been able to keep in touch with my friends. At that age it would also have been quite fun, I think. You know, FaceTiming and sending photos and songs and stuff.

When we first went on tour after I'd joined the band we must have been away for about eight or nine weeks. And there were no mobiles or anything. If I wanted to contact a somebody it would either have to be by a landline (although fat chance if we were abroad in those days) or by letter and, when you're on tour, you don't have time to write letters. I know I must sound like a bit of an old woman with all this 'back in my day' stuff, but it's all true. And it wasn't all *that* long ago either.

On the other side of the coin, social media can be quite harmful when it comes to friendships, as it tends to bring out the worst in us. Not all of the time, but if I had a pound for every time I'd seen somebody I know on social media making out that they're the happiest person on Earth when I know it's bollocks, I'd be able to hire a thera-pist every day for the rest of my life, which is what I'll probably need one day, thanks to social media!

What social media has done is bring out a competitive streak in some people, and friends of such folk generally fit into one of three camps. You'll get people like me who either just ignore or feel sorry for the competitive types, people who do the same as their posing friends and will try and go one better or people who, sadly, believe it all and get depressed because they're not living what they believe is such a wonderful life. What I always say to people in that latter situation is they should realise that ten seconds after that amazing-looking photo was taken of that person and this perfect family doing something cool, they'll either have had a massive row or their kids will have started punching the crap out of each other.

'It's all for show!' I say to them.

There is no such thing as a perfect family and the people who go to the biggest effort to try and prove that they have a perfect family are more than likely the ones with the biggest issues. There is actually a serious side to this, as it can make people feel incredibly lonely sometimes. It shouldn't, but it does. They're the people I feel sorry for and they suffer from a side of social media that I don't like. Or should I say a side of humanity that I don't like. Once again, I'm confusing who or what is actually to blame here.

Before social media, if somebody wanted to brag about how amazingly bright their children were or what kind of car they were currently driving, they'd have had to either ring everybody up one by one or take out an advert in a newspaper. Now they can bore the tits off people en masse on Facebook or whatever. Whoopee! I totally get it if you're sending this information to family or close friends. I mean, why wouldn't you? That's the joy of social media. Where it goes wrong though is when people start assuming that *everyone* they know on social media wants to read the news. In that situation, you're either a self-obsessed prat with no self-awareness or you're trying to make somebody jealous. Or depressed. Or both!

The way I like to keep in touch with my friends and family is via text. That's my chosen method of communication. The reason I prefer texting to talking on the phone is that you don't have to stop what you're doing. Or, at least, I certainly can't do two things when one of them is being on the phone. I tried having a conversation the other day while I was trying to persuade one of my cats to eat a tablet and the two actions became intertwined. It was actually a conversation about this book and, halfway through a sentence, I suddenly shouted, 'JUST EAT THE TABLET YOU FAT ILL BASTARD!' Luckily, I was talking to somebody who knows what I'm like so it wasn't a problem. In fact, it was quite funny, really, and they laughed like a drain! Equally, because of the job I do, which involves me having to talk, sometimes I just don't want to when I'm relaxing, so I text. A lot!

Can I be honest with you? One of the other reasons I text is through pure laziness; sometimes I just can't be arsed to talk. If I answered the phone every time one of my best friends called, I know for a fact that I'd be on there for at least an hour and if I've been talking all day for work, I just can't do it. I have to be in the mood for long telephone calls and, because I'm usually not in the mood, I text instead. It's not just my friends though. I ignore my family's phone calls too! My kids are always telling me off for it. The other day Ciara said to me, 'Mum, I've tried calling you four times. Why won't you just pick up the phone?' What I usually do in that situation is say to myself, 'I'll call them back in five minutes,' but I never do. I'm rubbish!

The way I try and sell it to my friends is by saying that I might not call them very often, but I'll text them all day if I can! And I will, believe me. I've been addicted to texting ever since I first got a mobile phone and because of the amount of practice I've had, I should really have the some of the fastest fingers in the world: mmm, I'm afraid not. I text like a blind, arthritic ninety-year-old with fat fingers and I always have. I'm absolutely in awe of my children when I watch them texting. They can be having a conversation with me and not looking at their phones while texting at the same time. I mean, how amazing is that? In fact, why don't I put it on social media and impress everyone? I'll come straight to the point though and say that my kids are better than everyone else's because they can talk and text. That'll ruffle a few feathers!

Sometimes, while I'm sitting there in awe, I'll ask Ciara to send a message for me. 'Why can't you send it?' she always asks.

'Because you're five times as fast as I am! Here,' I say, chucking her my phone. 'I'll say it, you type it.' It's the closest I've ever come to having my own secretary. She's very efficient though. At least fifty words a minute!

One of the most common questions I'm asked about friendship is if it's more difficult making friends when you're famous. Instead of just saying, 'Yes,' as people expect, I always say that it *can* be more difficult making friends when you're famous. The dilemma famous people have is whether somebody is being friendly with them because they like them or because they're famous – and it can be an issue sometimes. But, providing you keep your wits about you, you should be able to whittle out the people who are genuine from the fame-hungry and it's not nearly as difficult as it might be if you're painfully shy, for instance, or have a condition like Asperger's.

I'll tell you one thing being famous does give you – it makes it easier to meet people. Whether they're genuine or not you won't know immediately but it's a great introduction. Or, should I say, it can be! If you're famous the chances are some people you meet will already have formed an opinion about you. The main problem you face in this situation is that the opinion they've formed might well be negative, in which case you'll be starting on the back foot. Equally, it could be positive, in which case you'll be fine. Either way, the chances are that the people you meet will know more about you than you do about them and, for some people, that can be disconcerting.

Not me though. I don't give a stuff really. I wear my heart on the sleeve – always have – and if somebody walks up to me and says that they're sorry about my marriage ending or ask me how things are going on Tinder, I'll chat away. I'm very trusting, you see, and I try not to ask myself what their motives might be. After all, who says they have any motives? If I saw somebody I knew from the telly and I wanted to have a chat with them, I'd go over and try and have one. They might tell me to piss off, but so what? And what would my incentive be? My incentive would be that I fancied having a chat with that person. Simple as that! If we went through life wondering and worrying about what people's motives were when we met them, we'd all be friendless.

What I actually find harder than this is meeting people that I might like but have nothing in common with. That can be a bit awkward sometimes and it happens all the time, both in showbiz and in real life too. Thinking about it, I've hardly got any showbiz friends. Strange, isn't it? People often assume that the easiest people to meet and make friends with when you're famous are other famous people, but that's not the case, in my experience. I think people assume that you don't need to worry about whether your famous friend is being genuine, but I don't think that is necessarily true. Famous or not, people are people and you'll either get on with them or you won't. If they're only being nice because you're famous and you've got sod all in common, it'll become apparent at some point and you'll drop them like a hot potato. Just go with the flow and don't worry too much about it, that's my motto.

I tend to surround myself with people who aren't in the business. I don't do it consciously. It just happens. I always feel more comfortable in their company for some reason. You see, at the end of the day, I'm a working-class girl who's had a slightly different upbringing to most people and has a bit of a strange job, but those facts have had next to no bearing on who I am as a person. I have never, ever felt like a celebrity. I might be one in some people's eyes, if you have to use the word, but I've never felt like one.

Seriously, if you gave me a choice of going to a big, red-carpet event in London with a load of celebrities and the great and the good, or a party at somebody's house with a load of mad gossipy women who are probably all going to drink too much, I'd choose the party every time. As long as I can drink tea if I want and pop outside for a fag every now and then, I'd be as happy as a pig in you-know-what.

Ninety per cent of my friends are ordinary, working-class women like me and I'm very, very lucky to have them. We have an affinity, you see. A bond. And it's nothing to do with the class thing. There are no chips on any of our shoulders, thank you very much. We are who we are. It's one of the reasons why I get on so well with anyone I meet. There's no doubt about that.

One of the other things that draws me to people like this is that I've always craved normality. For all my claims about being and feeling ordinary there's no escaping the fact that my life hasn't always been that, yet it's what I've always yearned for. I guess it's no different to people who haven't experienced fame but want to know what it's like. You always want what you haven't got, don't you? It's human nature.

Every year the people at ITV send us really posh gifts from Fortnum & Mason and, when they arrive, I always say, 'Why the hell are you wasting all that money on me? Do I look like somebody who would shop at Fortnum & Mason? I can't even read or pronounce most of the labels!' My neighbours must think I'm as posh as hell, rolling out of a taxi carrying all this stuff. 'Coleen's been to Fortnum's again. She's so refined.' Yeah, like sugar!

I don't know if you remember, but years ago I used to do the Iceland adverts and at the end of every shoot they'd send me off with a really expensive bottle of champagne. After the third or fourth time I said to them, 'Look, I really do appreciate you doing this but don't get me champagne. That stuff's wasted on me.'

'OK,' they said, 'is there anything in particular you do like?'

'Oh, I don't know,' I said. 'Something that you think is a bit more me.'

Do you know what they got me after the next shoot? A giant bottle – a blue WKD! I pissed myself when they gave it to me and, although I wouldn't usually, I sat and drank the whole thing. I was hammered!

The majority of people I know who work in television but aren't celebrities (or execs) couldn't give a shit whether I'm famous or not. They might treat you differently if you are, but that's because they have to. In the end, then, do you know who I feel sorry for the most in this sort of situation, of potentially not knowing who wants to be your friend and who wants to kiss your arse? TV execs. I know, shock-horror! Me feeling sorry for a TV exec? Who'd have thought it? But when you're an exec *everybody* wants to kiss your arse, basically. From the stars to their agents.

You see, rightly or wrongly, TV execs hold a massive amount of power and, regardless of how uncomfortable it might make you feel, keeping on their right side and doing a bit of arse-licking from time to time might well be the difference between being in or out of work. If you feel uncomfortable though, there's a chance that the exec will feel even worse. I've been at parties where TV executives have literally been surrounded by ten or twenty people. Not people who want an autograph or a selfie. That's easy-peasy. No, these hangers-on want to be employed by the exec to further their careers. Some execs seem to revel in it and have obviously managed to cut themselves off emotionally, at least from the people who are harassing them. For others, it's not so easy. Either way, one of the reasons I never go near TV executives, unless I have to, is that I know for a fact that, if I walked up to one at a party, the first thing they'd think is, I wonder what she wants? That's definitely held me back in my career and if Melanie, my brilliant manager, could change anything about me – professionally, that is – I'd put money on it being able to schmooze.

I remember standing outside the old ITV studios once, having a fag, when I got chatting to this man. I had no idea who he was but we ended up having a right natter about life, mainly. Just then Ant and Dec walked past us and went into the studios. I always get a bit starstruck when I see them and I remember nudging this man and telling him how much loved them. A few minutes later we said our goodbyes and off he went back into the building. I followed a minute or so later and was stopped by somebody I knew.

'What were you talking to him about,' she asked curiously.

I thought, Mind your own bloody business! 'We were just talking rubbish, really,' I said to her. 'Why? What's up?'

'You do know he's one of the most powerful people at ITV?' she said.

'Oh, shit, is he?' I quickly went back over our conversation to see if I could remember whether or not I'd said anything embarrassing or incriminating. I didn't think I had, apart from mentioning how false the business could be sometimes. He agreed with me though! I bet he thought I was the cleaner. He certainly never offered me a job!

One of the most important things about friendship is laughter. It's one of the first things I notice about people and, if they make me laugh it's always a great start. It's the same when it comes to men. Unlike the Spice Girls, if you want to be my lover you've got to make me piss myself laughing first. Then you can get with my friends! That's my rule, I'm afraid, and it doesn't take much to set me off. Make me laugh, put the kettle on and you're in!

Some of the Loose Women are hilarious. Brenda Edwards, for instance, makes me die laughing and so does Ruth Langsford. They're people who, if I finished *Loose Women* tomorrow, I'd remain friends with for the rest of my life.

In order to look after a friendship though, first and foremost, you have to be honest. The thing that completely turned me off the friend at the stables who dropped me wasn't the fact that she stopped talking to me, it was the fact that she couldn't be honest with me. That's what cut me off. Had she told me what was wrong, the chances are we could have sorted it, but she didn't. She tried to make out that everything was fine, when it quite obviously wasn't. It's a shame when things like that happen, but friendships can only work when both people are honest. Otherwise, they're not worth bothering with. As with any relationship, it's all about communication.

In the past I've been guilty of bottling things up and hiding them from friends and it's never ended well. The friendships I lost were dear to me and it's one of my few regrets in life. In fact, I'm adamant that, had I said something, they'd still be in my life and I'd ask you, please, don't make the same mistakes I did. Whether it's a bestie or a sibling, if you value that relationship, then don't let anything fester. It's not just you you're in danger of upsetting, it's them too. You have to be tactful, of course (because I'm the queen of tactfulness!). If you have a problem with how a friend has behaved, don't sit them down and say, 'You've been a bit of a tosser. What are you going to do about it?' Think about how you're going to handle it first, then sit them down and call them a tosser!

Another thing I'd say is, try not to be too needy. Sometimes, if you have a really good friend, it's tempting to lay everything at their door, but that's not fair. I suppose

90

it's a compliment really, but if your friend's a bit of a softy they probably won't say anything and, as well as jeopardising your friendship long-term, you could be making their life a misery. That's why talking is so important. Not about you, necessarily, but about both of you. Every now and then, take a step back and look at how you are with your friends. Do you know what's going on with them? Or are you just emptying all your problems onto them? And vice versa – if a friend is using you and not giving anything back then that could be just as much of a problem.

Just remember that a good friendship needs looking after and is always worth fighting for. And friendship needs to be a two-way street!

. . . But you can't choose your family!

I've experienced so much over the years in the name of friendship, whether it be making friends, losing friends, helping friends, being helped by friends or just enjoying their company. And I include family in that. A big chunk of what makes a family tick is friendship and, if you don't get on with a relative, you're unlikely to want to spend time with them. It's the basis of any successful relationship and should be looked after as well as treasured.

Despite there being so many of us Nolans, generally we've always been very close, apart from a four-year period when I didn't speak to Anne or Denise. The three of us look back on that time now and wonder what the hell we were doing. It was all down to stubbornness, in the end, and I think it was losing our sister Bernie that made us see sense. Two well-known proverbs spring to mind here: 'Life's too short' (which it is) and, 'There's no fool like an old fool'. Or, in this case, three of them!

What connects us Nolans and keeps us close, apart from the fact that we're family, is the fact that we've experienced so much together. I could spend literally years reminiscing about what me and my family have been through together

– good and bad. It'd make a good film, actually! Penélope Cruz would obviously play me, although she might be a bit old now.

You hear so many horror stories about families who end up hating each other and that's always been a fear of mine. With there being so many of us and with us all having very different personalities, it could easily have gone tits up but, as it has turned out, there's always been more that binds us together than separates us. Granted, we've had to go looking for the common ground once or twice – as we did when me and my sisters fell out – but, in my experience, that becomes easier as you get older and boy, are we all older! Well, they are. I'm still the baby of the family.

I know friends can be closer than family – it's often that way around – but I think that, whatever happens with your friends, your family should always be your constant, really, and the ideal situation is to be close to your family and have a great group of friends. Fortunately, I'm in that situation and I consider myself to be incredibly blessed. It's true that you can choose your friends but not your family, which makes it even more important to make allowances if you have to and even say, 'Sorry' sometimes!

That time I fell out with Denise and Anne was one of the biggest family conflicts we've ever had. It was over nothing, really, and should have been sorted out within twenty-four hours, yet I didn't speak to Anne for about three years and Denise for four years. It all started after Anne and Ray had a row one day. The thing is, Anne and Ray always used to have rows and I'd lost count of the

times I'd said to them, 'Jesus, are you two arguing again?!'
An hour later they'd always be friends again – it was just
something that happened.

One day they had an argument while I was away and,
when I got back the next day, they still weren't talking to
each other. Each of them said to me that it would probably all blow over but, before it could, other people got
involved and it went completely stratospheric. Texts began
flying around and people started saying things that they
couldn't really take back. It was awful.

Unfortunately, this didn't just affect the people involved.
It affected everyone. If a family gathering was taking place
we'd receive a phone call to say that Anne and Denise
were going so I'd offer not to go. Everything became so
awkward. I think the worst thing was that Anne and Denise
missing my wedding. That really hurt – but we were all as
bad as each other.

And that's one of the reasons I always advise people to
communicate after a fall-out: I know how damaging it can
be when you don't. As a family, we always used to brush
everything under the carpet and our failure to communicate is probably what turned this row from being a storm
in a teacup, which is what it should have been, into a full-
scale family feud.

As is often the way, it took something incredibly sad to
bring us all to our senses and that was Bernie's death.
Everything was put into perspective after that and the
thought of continuing a battle that had been started over
something so trivial after she'd died would have been an

insult to her memory. Even then, things didn't get better overnight, but slowly the lines of communication started opening up again and I'm happy to report that we're all closer now than we've ever been. These days, if there's even a sniff of a fall-out with a member of my family I'll nip it in the bud and the others are exactly the same. Never again.

Because we're all busy people and because I live about seventy miles away from them, I don't get to see my family as often as I'd like these days. We do have a family WhatsApp group which, if I'm being honest, can be an absolute pain in the arse sometimes. They'll be on it all bloody day, talking crap, and my phone must ping at least twenty times an hour.

'Are any of you going to Asda?' one of them will say.

'No, but I'm going to Tesco,' will come the reply.

'Ooh, would you mind getting me some Cheddar? Theirs is much nicer.'

I sit there thinking, Just bloody phone each other, will you? The fact that I never phone anyone or even answer the bloody thing doesn't count, of course.

Despite the fact that we don't see each other that often, if I was in a bad place tomorrow, every single member of my immediate family would be here like a shot. Given the fact that they're all such strong people, that's actually quite a comforting realisation. And empowering. Seriously, as soon as anything happens in our family – to any of us – we just appear, like ants!

Do you know? I'm going to break the habit of a lifetime now and, instead of starting with my sisters – who I'm very close to but who are all well-known in their own right – I'm going to talk about my brothers, Tommy and Brian, for a change! The amount of people who don't even know I have two brothers is shocking really. Then again, they've always kept themselves to themselves, although they are both musicians and were part of the family act back in the 1960s and 1970s. I actually feel a bit guilty that we don't talk about them more than we do because they're both fantastic.

When we moved to London, when I was nine, Tommy and Brian decided to stay in Blackpool as they were both happily engaged at the time. Looking back, I think Brian regretted the decision for a while. Neither of the engagements lasted the course, unfortunately, and I think he wondered what might have been for his career if they had moved down with us. Him and Tommy are such good musicians– so who knows? He's happy now, though, which is the main thing.

Me and Tommy have always had a bit of a bond. Perhaps it's because he's the oldest and I'm the youngest? He'll whisper things in my ear sometimes – rude things, usually – and say, 'Don't tell your sisters!' They then hear me howling with laughter and say, 'What's so funny? Come on, tell us!'

Even though he lives in Blackpool, like me, Tommy has a life outside the town and he tends to dip in and out. He's so dry though and so funny. Neither of us give a shit, really. We're like two peas in a pod. Then again, musically we're very different. Tommy always liked heavy rock and heavy metal whereas the rest of us were Sinatra fans. He even had the long hair and the big moustache. My dad always used to shake his head and say, 'I don't know where we got him from.' When me and my sisters did a song with hard-rocker Lemmy from Motörhead, Tommy was very impressed. I don't think my dad was! Then again, Tommy was never one to want to come and meet these people. As I said, he's always kept himself to himself.

Brian's always been the sensible one. I know, a sensible Nolan? Shock, horror! There has to be one, I suppose. Despite Tommy being the oldest, Brian was always the one who'd tell him off – not my parents! He's got such a brilliant command of the English language and can cut you down with one sentence. He's done it to me loads of times over the years. I'll say something to him that he doesn't agree with and he'll come back at me with a sentence that either proves me wrong or just baffles me. My counter-argument approach, based on the fact that I'm not as clever as he is, is always, 'Aww, fuck off, Brian!' to which he always replies, 'And that's my point.' Bastard!

When we were touring the UK back in the 1980s, Brian and Tommy used to sell the merchandise at gigs. That meant that they both came on the tour bus, which was nice. It was all of us together again. Their other job on tour was to make us all laugh and they never disappointed. What I wouldn't give to do that again.

I am sometimes asked if there's a difference between the relationship I have with my brothers and the relation-ship I have with my sisters and the truth is I have a different relationship with all of them. Take my word for it, no two Nolans are the same, and I honestly wouldn't have it any other way.

Actually, there is probably a difference between my relationship with Tommy and Brian and my relationship with the girls. Although we talk about all kinds of different things, the foundation of my relationship with the boys has always been humour and it's something I treasure. When I think back to us growing up, I don't know how they managed. Imagine being stuck in a small terraced house with six hormonal women! It should actually be used as a punishment. I sentence you to ten years with the Nolan Sisters!

Even when we became famous, Brian and Tommy were never anything other than supportive, where some people might have been resentful. Knowing that they're there for us all has always been a great source of comfort and, even though I'm older and more resilient, that hasn't changed one bit.

The only person I know who loves having two big brothers as much as I do is Ciara. In fact, her relationship with Shane and Jake probably isn't dissimilar to my relationship with Brian and Tommy; there's a lot of laughter involved and they're protective of her as she's by far the youngest. The fact that the three of them get on so well is one of the things I'm always grateful for, every day, as there are obviously no guarantees. I just hope it lasts!

(Not) Coping with modern life

Being famous is a bit of a double-edged sword, really, but it isn't something I'd ever complain about. At least, not publicly!

Everything in life has pluses and minuses and keeping the minuses to a minimum, if you're famous, is as much about how you see yourself as how other people see you. What I mean by that is that you can't take yourself too seriously. Famous or not, I think this is good advice for anyone anywhere. I obviously can't mention any names (unfortunately!) but I could fill Wembley Stadium two or three times over with the number of famous people I've met over the years who've had their heads up their bums. I've been on *Celebrity Big Brother*, remember – twice! Honestly, though, I can smell people like that a mile off and I avoid them like the plague – unless I'm locked in a house with them. Come to think of it, I'm exactly the same with people who aren't famous but also have their heads up their bums! There's nothing more off-putting.

Work is obviously a really important part of anyone's life. My work just happens to involve being in the public eye, which comes with its good and bad points. At the end of the day though, it is my job and, as long as I enjoy doing it and people are willing to employ me – I'll carry on. If they don't, I'll just become a pygmy-goat farmer or something.

The first time I realised that me and my sisters might be famous was when I was about nine years old. We were invited to appear on *It's Cliff Richard* and after that the floodgates just opened. Everywhere we went people would want an autograph or a chat. Back then, shows like that would regularly get over twenty million viewers a week, which is unheard of these days. My parents would never have allowed me to become arrogant or conceited and, to be honest with you, I didn't feel any different. I'd been performing on stage with my family since the age of two and although the attention we received after appearing on TV was much greater, I'd been experiencing a version of it all my life. I don't mean that in a big-headed way. I just had a bit of a strange childhood!

What happened before things went bananas was like an apprenticeship and it allowed us all to take fame in our stride. At least, more than we would have had we not already been in the business. I suppose the only downside to growing up in the public eye – at least, from my own point of view – was that, because it had all been normal-ised, I never got to have those dreams about appearing on *Top of the Pops* that all my friends had. That's why, when people ask me what it was like appearing on shows like *Top of the Pops* at such a young age I usually disappoint them. They're expecting me to say how excited I was, but I wasn't. I was just doing as I was told. I'm not saying I didn't enjoy it – I did. It just wasn't that exciting.

A more popular question is have I always been ambitious? Once again, whoever's asking that question won't get the answer they were expecting. The fact is, you see, I've never been ambitious. At least, not about showbusiness. Appearing on *It's Cliff Richard* just happened, as did having a No. 1 single and selling millions of records. It might have been different for my sisters as they were older, but I was just doing as I was told. I never thought about it, the same as I never went to bed thinking, Ooh, I hope we get to No. 1. In fact, my only ambition when I was a teenager was to become a vet. That's what I used to dream about; not going on *Top of the Pops* or being asked for my autograph.

The only thing that stopped me from pursuing a career as a vet was the fact that I'm lazy. That was the main reason I joined up with my sisters – I couldn't be arsed to put the work in. A-levels and then five years at university? No, thank you very much! I'm not joking. I did not have any dreams about becoming a professional singer whatsoever. It was the only thing I was any good at.

If you're not lazy, I would encourage you to give your dreams a shot. Looking back at the younger me, had I not gone into the family business, so to speak, I'd either have had a go at becoming a vet or got some other kind of job working with animals. When it comes to choosing a career, I'd say you should think about what you're passionate about and what you're good at and work out if there's a job to be had there. Then work out what you need to do to get to that place and whether it's achievable. If it isn't, think of something else that is. Experiencing rejection or failure can easily stifle your self-confidence and, despite rejection being a potentially giant obstacle, learning to get over it could be one of the most important things you ever do. That's the same advice I give to my kids. Work like hell to realise your dreams and, if it doesn't work out, keep on trying. Never lose sight of them, that's the main thing.

As for my own family, once the television started we had to move from Blackpool to London and that's where I went to school. I moved back to Blackpool for a couple of years and, at fifteen, I left school to join my sisters. I was meant to have a tutor for a year until I was sixteen but she never turned up. Naturally, I was devastated!

Speaking of tutors. One of my favourite memories from those early days is going on a tour to South Africa for six weeks when I was ten. Because I was still at school I had to have a tutor (this one turned up!). Fortunately, she was lovely and I didn't mind one bit. We played gigs all over the country and what I remember most are the animals. We went to Kruger National Park for a few days and I saw elephants, giraffes, zebras, leopards and rhinos. For a ten-year-old animal lover with ambitions of becoming a vet it was a dream come true. Gigs? What gigs?

The closest I've ever come to being overwhelmed by being famous was when we made it in Japan. At the time we'd sold more records in that country than The Beatles and we've gone on to sell over twenty-five million. What we experienced in Japan was wasn't fame, though. It was mania! We were followed by literally thousands and thousands of people and had police escorts wherever we went. I think what endeared us to the Japanese people was the fact that we were sisters. They're very family orientated over there and we just seemed to capture their imaginations. They also know a good tune when they hear one, and we were also ridiculously talented, of course! Don't forget that.

The only problem we had with being so popular in Japan was that the country isn't exactly around the corner; getting out there and making the most of it was an issue. One of ways we remedied this was taking part in the first live pop concert from the UK to Japan. We did it from Trafalgar Square and apparently the entire country watched it. Well, most of them.

That whole Japan experience was probably what stopped me from being quite so blasé about being famous and I went from my status not really registering to thinking, Wow, this is fun! What the hell happened there? That said, I do remember thinking, when we were over in Japan, that all I wanted to do was go home and go out with my mates. That's the thing about being in the public eye. People sometimes assume that it's a non-stop party and that you never stop enjoying yourself, but that's rubbish. You're either working your bum off or sitting around waiting to work your bum off. I'm not complaining, though. I'm not afraid of hard work (sometimes!) and I can amuse myself quite easily if the need arises. I'm low maintenance.

Live. Laugh. Love.

I've also never known any different – if you put me in a nine-to-five situation I probably wouldn't last two minutes. Actually, I'd be an absolute liability! Can you imagine me working in an office with lots of other women. How much work would I get done? Oh, my God, it'd be a disaster. I'd be sacked within a day!

Funnily enough, because I work on *Loose Women* and I was in a female band people probably assume that I'm a staunch feminist and believe in female camaraderie etc. Wrong! I find women really hard work sometimes – especially these days. Take the whole thing about manners. If a man opens a door for a woman, it's supposed to be insulting now because, by doing so, he's somehow claiming that she's incapable of doing it herself. What a load of utter bollocks! If a man allowed a door to close in my face I'd probably call him a bastard and I'd do exactly the same if it was a woman. Seriously, when did being polite suddenly become a crime? If people can be offended by somebody opening a door for them, whether it be a man, a woman or a pink bloody elephant, then they should stay indoors and never go out again. Do I think there's still a lot of sexism around? Absolutely, I do, but opening doors for people isn't part of it.

The thing about me is that, despite me having had an unconventional childhood and despite me having spent most of my life in the spotlight, I'm actually just dead normal, really. Most people would have given their eye teeth to sell squillions of records in Japan and be as famous as we were, yet all I wanted to do was go home, see my friends and go to the pub. The fame bit's great but I can only enjoy that if I've got the other bit sorted out. And I think that's true whatever line of work you're in. Work to live, not live to work! The thing is, I'd never yearn for fame as much as I yearn for normality. No way. I can take or leave being famous, yet normality is a necessity for me. I need to feel normal. I don't need to feel famous.

One of the most positive things about me having such an unconventional upbringing is that when it came to my own kids I made sure they had the opposite. I think anyone in my situation would have done the same thing. In fact, I was more passionate about them having a normal and well-balanced childhood than I have been about any job I've ever done. I also wanted to be there for everything. Every parents' evening, every sports day, every school play. The lot. In my entire school career I think I did about two sports days – and I used to love sports when I was little. It was even worse with parents' evenings. In fact, I don't think my mum and dad came to one, but for no other reason than they were working. Actually, so was I.

I'm not having a go at my mum and dad but I do remember being disappointed that they didn't go to parents' evenings. I wanted them to see my work, speak to my teachers and be dead proud of me. When I had kids of my own the memories of this came flooding back and I vowed not to make the same mistake. I also wanted to see how they were getting on and watch them progress, of course. To me, that's one of the best things about being a parent. I wasn't doing it out of a sense of duty!

Live. Laugh. Love.

When all three of my kids got to two years old I couldn't help remembering that, when I was that age, instead of being put to bed at seven o'clock like normal kids, I would usually be on my way to somewhere like Glasgow with my family to do four spots in a working man's club! And there were no hotels to check into afterwards. We'd drive home and, regardless of what time we got in, we'd have to get up at the usual time and carry on as normal. It was like another world and, although I'm not decrying it, I just couldn't imagine for a minute me doing the same with my kids. I'd have social services on me like a shot!

Once again, I don't want this to sound big-headed but, when I was recording *Piers Morgan's Life Stories* in 2021 and they started playing all those clips from when I was nine or ten, like *The Harry Secombe Show*, I kept on thinking to myself, God, I've done a lot of stuff! It's funny, though, because when they first asked me to do the Piers Morgan programme, as well as being thrilled, the first thought that came into my head was, Blimey! That's going to be a boring hour. What have I done?

When I got to the studio, all of the production team started saying things like, 'You've had a bit of a life, haven't you?' I remember thinking to myself, They're just being nice! Then Piers came up and said, 'I cannot get over the life you've had, Coleen!' Even then I just didn't get it and it was only when we started recording the show and playing the clips that it started to hit home.

The response I got after the show was broadcast was nothing short of amazing and, by then, I was happy to admit that perhaps I have had quite an interesting life. My kids put it slightly differently. If I've been on TV or something one of them will say, 'Mum, you do realise you've had a really weird life!' What actually drives them to say that I'm not entirely sure but I always go, 'Leave me alone! I don't know any different!'

It has been weird, though, if you think about it. I was born into a family who were nicknamed the 'Blackpool Von Trapps' and I was on stage – usually very late at night – from the age of two. By the age of nine I'd become a TV star, together with the rest of my family, and by the age of fifteen we'd had a No. 1 single in God knows how many countries and had become mega-stars in Japan. After that, we did that single with Lemmy, who complimented me on my boobs, before having a load more hits and releasing an album that spent thirty-three weeks on the UK chart. A few years later I met Shane, got married, had Shane Jr and Jake, got divorced, became a bit sad, felt better, reinvented myself as a TV presenter (or big gob!) and an agony aunt, met Ray, had Ciara, got married to Ray after Ciara was born (whoops!), went on *Celebrity Big Brother*, almost killed Julie Goodyear and came second, went back on *Celebrity Big Brother* and won before almost having a nervous breakdown, fell out of love with Ray, felt sad, then divorced Ray, felt happy, moved house, bought three pygmy goats, felt even happier and – here we are! If all that didn't leave its mark on me I don't know what would have done. It's a wonder I'm not in a straitjacket! (I'll be having a fitting soon, most probably.)

I'm sometimes asked what the best and worst things about being famous are and my answer usually changes, depending on what kind of mood I'm in. Well, it changes when it comes to thinking of the worst things! From memory, the last time I was asked the question I said that the best thing about being famous was people being nice to you. I don't care who you are, everybody has an ego and everyone likes having their feathers stroked occasionally. It's even better when I meet people who I've helped via the problem page or TV. To know that you've made a difference to somebody's life is wonderful, but to then be told by the person you've helped is just amazing. There is no better feeling in the whole world, believe me. Whatever job you happen to do, whether you're a primary school teacher or work in a supermarket, knowing you've made a difference is a feeling that can't be beaten.

To be given the opportunity to actually do that in the first place makes me feel very grateful indeed, and I've been doing it for twenty years! What's also really nice is when people come up and say that they enjoy watching me on *Loose Women* or like listening to 'I'm in the Mood for Dancing'. It's the gift that keeps on giving and I always love talking to people who want to talk to me.

I actually can't remember what I've said was the worst thing about being famous but the one that springs to mind now (apart from trolls, who – as well as being extremely sad people – can be an absolute pain in the arse sometimes) is going through something that, if you weren't famous, you wouldn't want anyone to know about. If you're famous it all comes out eventually, whether you want it to or not, and it's often just a case of practising damage limitation.

As opposed to trying to hide these things, which would only be possible for so long, I tend to embrace the inevitability of it all and wear my heart on my sleeve. What's the point of fighting something if you're not going to win? I'm not saying this makes it all perfect but, if you're going through a traumatic time and are in the public eye, the sooner you get it out in the open the sooner it'll go away. That's the idea, anyway! My trouble is that, once I've started talking about something I don't stop; instead of being forgotten about, the headlines get bigger and bigger! That does leave me open to a certain amount of intrusion and ridicule by the press but it's more than worth it. It doesn't bother me, nor should it you if you're going through something similar.

Second only to never losing sight of your dreams, I'd say the most important piece of general advice I could give anybody – especially with social media being as popular as it is – is to take other people's opinions and judgements with a large pinch of salt, whether that be in a professional environment or a personal one. If I took every comment or insult to heart I'd be in a psychiatric ward for the rest of my life!

Some people assume that when Shane and Jake started showing an interest in entering showbusiness I'd have tried to steer them away, but not a bit of it. When it came to Jake, I would have been a lot more alarmed and shocked if he had not gone into showbusiness; from the age of about two he was obsessed by it. He never went through that stage of wanting to be a policeman or an astronaut – and even I went through that. Jake always wanted to be either an actor or a singer and he was always very interested in what Shane Sr and I did for a living.

By contrast, I was actually quite surprised when Shane said that he wanted to go into showbusiness. He must have been about sixteen, which is quite late and, until then, he'd always been far more interested in football. He was scouted by quite a few teams as a youngster and even did some of his coaching badges over in America. It came out of the blue when he announced one day that he was going to audition for the school play. He's never done that before, I thought. Perhaps he's getting the bug? The part that Shane was going for was the lead in *Grease* – which his dad had played years earlier on a big tour of the UK – and he got it! After that he was hooked and he's never looked back.

Although I love the fact that Shane and Jake are in showbusiness, I worry about them all the time, as it's such a precarious industry. Now more than ever! I think I'm going to get the full set, though, as Ciara's started writing and recording songs. Her mum's a singer and her dad's a guitarist, so I suppose it was inevitable!

Showbusiness is a horribly cruel industry and that's something else that worries me about the kids, although Shane and Jake are both quite established now and have already had quite a bit of success. But I know only too well that you can be the most talented person on Earth and, if you don't get some luck along the way, the chances are you won't even get a sniff of success. In fact, if I had to put a percentage on things I'd say it's just twenty per cent talent and at least eighty per cent luck. Seriously! I've seen people with a thousand times more talent than anyone else who's made it, yet they have never got anywhere near making it big themselves.

It's different in other walks of life. Nine times out of ten, if you aren't good enough, you'll eventually get found out and there's no hiding place. Take sport, for instance. Can you imagine Ronaldo or Wayne Rooney playing for Macclesfield FC? I can't! (Mind you, that's probably because I hate football.) Of course it would never happen in sport – but it would in showbusiness. And has. Millions of times! I just hope that if Ciara does decide to make a go of it and is good, she at least gets the breaks to match. Fingers crossed.

People do sometimes write to me at the *Mirror* about this sort of thing and the advice I always give them is to support whatever dreams their kids have to the best of their ability and be there to guide them on another path if it doesn't work out. As a parent you can't do any more than that.

One thing I would never do is turn around to one of my kids and say, 'You shouldn't do that.' I might not always like what they're thinking of doing, but one of the worst things you can do to a child is trample on their dreams.

A couple of years ago, Ciara got a job in Superdrug and I was absolutely over the moon. Finally, I thought. One of my children is just going to have a normal, secure job! A few months later she came to me and said, 'Mum, I don't want to do this any more. I just want to write music.'

I said, 'OK,' went to bed, cried for ten minutes and I was fine. Actually, I wasn't that fine because while Ciara was working at Superdrug she got 40 per cent off and that all went out of the window. Why else do you think I went to see her almost every day she worked there? I wasn't just being sociable!

The biggest challenge I've ever faced professionally is having to reinvent myself after Shane and I split up. Actually, I didn't *have* to reinvent myself. I could have carried on being a full-time mum if I'd wanted and, had Shane and I not split up, I would probably have done just that.

What kicked everything off again was a TV show called *Celebrity Heartbreak*. It was presented by Trisha Goddard – no prizes for guessing what the format was; the clue's in the name! I forget who else was on the show but when they asked me if I'd like to talk about my experiences I thought, Yeah, why not? I've got nothing to lose. Except my dignity, of course!

My appearance led to an invitation to promote the show on *Loose Women*, which had recently started. I can't say I was really a fan of *Loose Women*, then, as it hadn't been going very long, but it was definitely becoming popular. It was nice to start making a few TV appearances, though.

I'd been a stay-at-home mum for the previous two years and, before it all went wrong between me and Shane, I'd even got myself a normal part-time job in a health food shop. I think I'd actually resigned myself to being a full-time mum and never going back to showbusiness. Or, at least not until the boys were settled at school. I don't mean I'd settled on that plan in a negative way. In fact, I was perfectly happy. Shane was doing really well, I had two beautiful boys. It was all perfect. Being a full-time mum is something that, even today, people decry and sometimes belittle, yet it genuinely is – or can be – one of the hardest jobs on the planet. Regardless of what you do or how much you get paid, if you lose a job outside the home for whatever reason the chances are you'd be able to find something else. If you're a full-time mum there isn't that option. You've got to stick to it, no matter what, and the responsibility of being entrusted with the care of small human beings, twenty-four-seven, weighs a lot heavier on my shoulders than running an office or being a panellist on a television show. I appreciate that people find work extremely stressful sometimes, but it still doesn't compare to being a full-time parent. No chance.

When the marriage went tits up, I went into survival mode and the upshot of that was saying 'Yes' to *Celebrity Heartbreak* and *Loose Women*. During the divorce hearing I remember the judge saying, 'At thirty-four years of age you are still young enough to find yourself a full-time job and start a new career,' and I remember thinking, But I've never had a bloody job! At least not the kind of job that the judge was referring to. It was actually pretty daunting at the time and when *Celebrity Heartbreak* came along, the opportunity felt like a godsend.

Live. Laugh. Love.

Appearing on *Loose Women* to promote the other show was great fun and I got on really well with everyone. I wish I could remember what I said. It can't have been anything too embarrassing as, a few weeks later, they asked if I'd like to come back on as a guest presenter one day. A return visit? 'Yes, please!' I said.

Pretty soon I was up and running and my quiet little domestic life was a distant memory. After I appeared on *Loose Women* a couple more times the producers asked if I'd like to become a regular presenter and the rest, as they say, is history!

Yet again, the situation that brought this opportunity to life was pretty horrible, yet it turned into something wonderful and I have literally spent twenty years mouthing off and having a laugh! There's no other way of putting it really, is there?

It's never too late to try something else, though. I've got a friend who spent twenty years as an accountant and, one day, he jacked it all in and started his own business. He suddenly realised one day that he didn't like being an accountant, but instead of just grinning and bearing it like many people probably would, he decided to back himself and try something new. He's not making anywhere near as much money but he's never been happier.

The people who were most surprised at me going into presenting were my sisters. 'Hang on,' said Maureen. 'Whenever we did interviews you were always the one who never said a word. And now you're a presenter? How the hell did that happen?' To be fair, she had a point. As a

Nolan Sister I was always the quiet one and they used to say to me afterwards, 'Will you bloody say something next time?' Me becoming a presenter, at least in my sister's eyes, was like Carol McGiffin becoming a nun. But when we were interviewed as the group, I was the youngest and a bit shy, although there was another reason I didn't say much – I could never get a flaming word in edgeways! I'm not joking. It was just pointless even trying sometimes; I'd just smile for the cameras and let them get on with it.

I'll tell you what I did do during those early years, and that's listen. I remember my sisters all going through break-ups and sobbing in the corner and I'd sit there thinking, That's never going to happen to me. I never ever voiced it but things like that were always running through my head and I learned a lot over the years.

Loose Women was probably the first time in my life when I was actually given a voice and the fact that I took to it in the way that I did was as much of a surprise to me as it was anyone else. Not because I wasn't confident about talking: I just didn't know, A, if I could do it in that environment and, B, if anyone would want to listen to me! I know loads of people who can talk for Britain but I wouldn't necessarily want to listen to them all, at least not on a regular basis. Realising that people did want to hear what I had to say – and still do, I hope – was an unexpected shot in the arm.

Interviewing is one thing, but I know I couldn't do public speaking. My manager, Melanie, is always calling me with offers to talk at lunches or conferences and I've never said 'Yes' to any of them. It drives her mad! Talking to a few million people through a television camera is, in my opinion, far less scary than the prospect of talking to a hundred people in a room somewhere. Honestly, you could offer me a million pounds and I still wouldn't do it.

Even on *Loose Women* I do feel that my confidence is tested to the point where I have to have a word with myself, such as when they dressed me up in a Christmas tree costume for our seasonal special. In these situations, I always have to say to myself, 'Come on, Col, what's the worst thing that can happen, apart from making a tit of yourself?' It wouldn't work with public speaking I'm afraid – that would require either a miracle or some drugs – but every time they want to dress me up as a bloody crayon or something, that mantra gets me into the costume.

The other thing, apart from public speaking, that not even my kids or my manager can convince me to do is appear on a game show. From the safety of my couch, I'm an absolute genius. In fact, I'm in awe of myself some-times when *Who Wants to Be a Millionaire?* is on and I've been known to get up to a hundred grand. If I had to do that for real in front of Jeremy Clarkson and he asked me what my name was, I wouldn't be able to tell him. And it wouldn't be a case of 'What doesn't kill you makes you stronger' – as in, I'd learn from it. It'd be a case of, 'What doesn't kill you makes you look like a thicko in front of millions of people.' No, thank you very much.

When I first joined *Loose Women*, back in 2000, you could pretty much voice whatever opinions you liked, whereas now you have to be so, so careful. As well as being at the

mercy of legal restrictions, if you say something that somebody on social media doesn't agree with you can end up
being hammered for it. In our morning meetings at *Loose
Women*, we'll discuss what we're going to talk about in case
a subject that, on the face of it, seems quite harmless, can
quickly turn into something taboo. Also, everything we're
going to discuss on the show has to be run by the legal
department first, just in case there's a danger of us dropping ourselves and ITV in it. It's quite stifling, to be honest.
Anyone would think we had a history of saying things we
shouldn't? Erm . . .

As an example, we had a subject on *Loose Women* the
other day: is it ever insulting to tell somebody when they've
lost weight or how good they look? I nearly fell off my
bloody chair when it was brought up. Apparently, by
suggesting that somebody might have lost weight or looks
good, you're suggesting that they used to be fat or didn't
look *as* good, which might hurt their feelings and offend
them. '*What?*' During the discussion, I said to Ruth that I
look better now because I've lost some weight and the
reason I look better is because I used to be fat. In fact, if
somebody doesn't acknowledge the fact that I've lost
weight and look better than I used to, I want to smash
their bloody face in! (Please don't take that seriously, by the
way. I don't really.)

Seriously though, when did people start to become
offended by everything? It didn't happen overnight.
Freedom of speech is slowly being eradicated because
people are desperate to be offended – and why are they

desperate to be offended? Because it turns them into a victim, which makes them the centre of attention. It's an ego trip, basically, and a very expensive one at that.

On the other side of the coin, what if I see somebody who's lost a lot of weight but didn't have to and looks ill? Am I supposed to ignore it, too, just in case I offend them? If I care about that person even a little bit I'll want to know what's happening just in case I can help, in the same way that I'd want to compliment somebody who looks good for having lost some weight. One of my sisters has just lost a stone and a half and if I hadn't mentioned to her she'd have punched me! Fortunately, the kind of people I'm friends with and am related to are not the terminally offended, but that wouldn't stop me from commenting on somebody who was only an acquaintance. If somebody looks fabulous, it's in my nature to tell them, and I'm not going to change that on the off-chance that they might be itching to take offence. I'm sorry, but you can stick that.

Correct or acceptable terminology seems to change every week these days and I don't know about you, but I have problems keeping up. All I can do is keep on listening and adapt if I think it's necessary and if I don't, I won't. It took me a long time to find my voice and I'm buggered if I'm going to keep quiet just in case I say the wrong thing. In fact, you could say I've made a living from saying the wrong thing! It's what I do best. I absolutely adore what I do for a living and have been very lucky to have been given a second crack at the whip.

Social (bloody) media

Let's have a look at social media for a bit because it's such a big part of our lives these days and such a big subject. If you're in the public eye, it's a necessary evil and I, like a lot of people my age – who aren't really that interested in it – have had to learn to get used to it and even try and enjoy it.

I remember when Facebook started. It was all funny videos at first and I used to quite enjoy it. After that Twitter became along, which I managed to resist for a year or two. I was worn down eventually and I must admit that, for the first few months, I enjoyed it. In fact, I was never off my phone.

I have absolutely no idea what happened but at some point Twitter started becoming quite toxic and, in my opinion, it's gone downhill ever since. My management still run my Twitter account day-to-day but I only go on very, very occasionally. Too many trolls, too many people desperate to be offended and too many idiots. It's just not for me, unfortunately, and I've instructed my management not to tell me if it all kicks off because of something we've said. My son Shane, on the other hand, absolutely loves

Twitter and he's always on there, rowing with somebody. Actually, I should get him to run my account. I wonder how that would end up?

I stopped using Twitter myself the day after my sister Bernie died. Somebody tweeted, 'I hope you die of cancer like your sister.' I'm far too long in the tooth to let something like that get to me but, at the same time, I'm not going to hang around and just take it. Some people said, 'Yeah, but they're only idiots. Ignore them.' It's not so much the content but the very fact that such trolls can contact me directly that is the problem. Would you give a complete stranger your mobile phone number? No, of course you wouldn't. Well, being on Twitter's almost the same and if you're OK with thousands of people being able to send you messages any time of day or night then you go right ahead.

I came off Facebook when people started posting videos of things like kids or animals being battered. I used to go to bed not being able to sleep. It was horrific. I know things like that happen but I sure as hell don't want to be reminded of it two or three times a day. Also, the fact that there are people out there who find things like that entertaining or even enjoyable is beyond the pale! I don't want to share a platform with people like that. It's bad enough sharing a planet with them!

The biggest worry I have about social media is the effect it has on kids. My kids, your kids, everybody's kids. I get why it can be so addictive but I also know how damaging it can be. Kids are already under such pressure these days to look a certain way or even to like a certain band or singer. It's frightening – and all driven by social media. And then you have online bullying, of course, which forms part of social media. I get hundreds of letters at the *Mirror* from parents who are worried about cyber-bullying and, in my opinion, not enough has been done over the years to protect kids. I hope it's starting to change.

When Facebook first came along Shane and Jake were just about old enough, and savvy enough, to handle it, but Ciara wasn't. She'd have been just a few years old when it became popular over here. She wasn't allowed a mobile until she was eleven and even then I used to monitor how long she spent on Facebook; I watched her like a hawk. Some of her friends had phones from the age of seven and, because kids always want what their friends have got, she felt left out. It made no difference to me and Ray though. What does a seven-year-old need a smartphone for? She would never be out on her own at that age. In fact, when those of her friends with mobiles came to our house, nine times out of ten they'd leave them at home; they didn't know what to do with them.

I remember sitting her down one day – this was after a twenty-minute pester session about getting a smartphone – and explaining exactly why I didn't want her to have one. I didn't say, 'You are not getting a smartphone, young lady!' I just gave her my reasons, which were based around me wanting to protect her. Kids aren't daft and quite often they'll go and process things after a conversation like that, which is exactly what Ciara did. The next time somebody asked her why she wasn't allowed a smartphone she said it was because her mummy loved her very much and wanted to protect her, which was the absolute truth. Kids don't want to be told that they're too young, even when they are. At seven they think they're fifteen, except you know they're not. Just being completely honest with them can make so much difference.

Instagram's good. That seems to be the app that most people in my world gravitate towards these days and I've had a lot of fun on there so far. It also offers you more control and the only people who can comment on my posts are people I've chosen to follow. I'm not going to follow a bloody troll now, am I? Everybody I follow on Instagram's absolutely gorgeous and, when a discussion starts after I've posted something, I know it's going to be a nice one. Unlike on Twitter where it would probably end up in a flaming pile on!

Getting back on the horse

You remember I said earlier that one of the worst things about being famous was the press covering traumatic events? Well, my own experience in this department came about a year after landing the job on *Loose Women* and it's still one of my lowest points of my entire career.

It was 2001 and, following my successful initial run on *Loose Women*, I was offered a job co-presenting *This Morning*, which was – and still is – one of the biggest shows on daytime TV. To cut a very long story short, I moved my entire family, including a newborn baby, from Blackpool to London only for *This Morning* to end up getting rid of me after just a few months. We had to sell the house, take the kids out of school and move back to Blackpool. My financial situation was very shaky. When I first got the job, I had wondered about buying a home in London and I was told to go ahead. They assured me I was going to be on the show for ever, or words to that effect. Nine months later I had been left with a big house in the capital city, a huge mortgage and no income. My saving financial grace was that I hadn't sold the house in Blackpool and at least we had somewhere to live when we moved back. That really was what preserved us and I don't know what we'd have done if I'd sold it. I came close but something stopped me going ahead. Almost like a sixth sense.

The effect this had on my self-esteem was crippling but what made it worse was the fact that the press had an absolute field day. Everywhere I looked I was reminded of the fact that, in some people on *This Morning*'s eyes, at least, I wasn't good enough. If that isn't enough to make you feel worthless and paranoid, I don't know what is.

Unfortunately, the immediate aftermath of me being sacked from *This Morning* was almost as damaging as the event itself and, for a time, work was hard to come by. We found it hard to make ends meet. I suppose I was damaged goods as far as some were concerned and the industry was going to make a collective decision, and in its own time, on whether or not I was for the scrapheap or worth employing again.

I ended up doing outside broadcasts for local TV for some fifty quid a day. Anything, just to keep my hand in and earn some cash. It was so, so demoralising – I can't tell you. To go from fronting the biggest show on British daytime television, five days a week, to doing the occasional outside broadcast on a local channel; it's a pretty big fall, really.

Once again, though, that's just the nature of the industry beast and if you can't take the bad times along with the good ones you won't last a week. I had to fight tooth-and-nail to come back from that; professionally, at least, it was one of the hardest things I've ever had to do. I had to go to work and smile in front of a television camera when all I'd been reading in the papers is that everyone thought I was crap. It was, at best, a bit weird and at worst just a demoralising pain in the bloody arse! What I also found hard – and this was an important lesson, really – was the fact that it's always the person in front of the camera who gets the blame. If it's their fault, fair enough, but there are so many occasions when the presenter isn't to blame, yet they're the first to go. Equally, as a presenter you can't go out and say whose fault it really is as you'd never work again and the public will just think you're bitter.

That was a hard time. Believe me, it was. I'd be reading something derogatory in the newspapers about me leaving *This Morning* and think, But that's not true! You're lying to the public and now they're going to hate me. All I wanted to do was let everybody know that ninety-nine per cent of what they were reading in the papers was absolute rubbish. The thing is, I didn't have a voice in that situation and unless I was going to go for the jugular and ruffle some feathers the press didn't want to know. And why would they? They need to sell newspapers and me asking their readers not to believe everything they read isn't going to do that. The journalists would have given anything to know who I personally blamed for having to leave because that would have caused conflict and conflict sells newspapers! And I would never have worked again, of course, if I'd done that.

One of the things that kept me going through all this was a voice in my head that kept saying, 'You can't give up,

Live. Laugh. Love.

Coleen. You have to keep going!' This was interrupted sometimes by another – less helpful – voice reminding me that just a few weeks previously I'd been in the job of my dreams earning a load of money, but the second voice never became the louder of the two. I wouldn't let it. The way to overcome that negative voice, in my experience, is to get your head down and just get on with it. Sometimes it isn't easy, but the choice is always yours and you've just got to back yourself. My kids have been helpful in this department and sometimes, when my confidence is low, they'll sit me down and say, 'You can do this, Mum. Seriously, you can!' That can make all the difference, sometimes.

I suppose the take-home message from this story, if there has to be one, is the same as many others in this book, which is to try and take positives from upsetting and negative situations and come back stronger. I've had to do that thousands of times during my professional and personal life and I'm sure the majority of you are the same. It's easier said than done, of course, but what choice do you have? I owed it to myself and to my family to stick two fingers up at what had just happened and come back stronger, and I did. It took a while to rebuild things but I managed it eventually.

Money, money, money

I've talked about fame as it comes with the job, and what goes hand and hand with fame? Fortune. But when it comes to my case, my first question would be, what bloody fortune?

The whole time I was a member of the Nolan Sisters I earned £165 a week. In fact, our band used to get more than us. They were all on eighty pounds a gig each and could earn the same as us in two days. Regardless of where we were in the world, or how many gigs we played, that was always what we got.

We certainly weren't the first band to be treated like this and there have probably been thousands more since. We made some awful decisions about how to manage our career and were looked after by people who didn't really know what they were doing. More than anything though, we were exploited. I mean, what kind of company offers you a contract lasting ten years and the money's the same at the end of the agreement as it was at the beginning? I still can't believe we signed it. Talk about naive!

To begin with, I was actually quite happy with the arrangement, but I was so young then. Even today, how many fifteen-year-olds do you know who earn £165 a week? And this was in 1980! Go forward a few years, however, and – despite us having sold twenty-five million records in Japan and millions more elsewhere – we were still on £165 a week. All of our contemporaries seemed to be buying nice houses and driving nice cars and we all thought, Hang on, something's not quite right here!

Had we taken more of an interest in the legal side of things and got ourselves an experienced manager then things could have been different. To be honest, we were just happy that a big record company wanted to sign us. They obviously knew that though and arranged the deal accordingly. Any manager worth their salt would have taken one look at it and said, 'They're trying to rip you off,' but we didn't have one. More fool us!

Anyway, that's all water under the bridge now. It would have been nice to walk away from it all with a Rolls-Royce, a big house and millions in the bank, but we didn't, did we? There's bugger all we can do about it now and one of the things I refuse to do is allow it to affect what we achieved, not to mention my memories of it. Some bands spend years and years trying to claw money back by dragging ex-managers or record companies through the courts. Can you imagine what that must do to you? I'm not saying that what happened to us didn't upset me, but I had to let it go. Some things are worth more than money and my sanity is definitely one of them!

So, what do you think I am then, a spender or a saver?

I'm not adverse to spending money, if I've got it. I just rarely spend it on conventional things, like jewellery or clothes. In fact, I never buy designer clothes. Ever! I'm definitely my mother's daughter in that respect. She used to buy her clothes from second-hand shops, even when we had money. I'm not as bad as that but if you looked at the label of an item of clothing I was wearing it'd be far more likely to have Florence & Fred written on it than Gucci. What's more, buying something I actually like from somewhere like Tesco or M&S will give me infinitely more pleasure than a five-hundred-pound Gucci belt. I just do not care about that kind of thing.

My two biggest weaknesses when it comes to spending money are the animals and the kids. I love spending money on them. In fact, sometimes they tell me off for it. 'Mum,' they say. 'Will you please just spend it on yourself!' I've never spoiled the kids, but if they need something and I can help them get it, then I'm in there straight away. In fact, nothing gives me greater pleasure.

You sometimes hear people who are mega-rich say things like, 'I don't give my children anything. They can stand on their own two feet!' Whenever I hear that I always think to myself, Why have you had kids, then? If you're in a position to be able to help your kids when they need it – or even treat them occasionally – why on earth wouldn't you? There are probably hundreds of millions of parents around the world who would give their eye teeth to be able to help the people they love but who never get the opportunity. And I can't imagine saying to my children, 'By the way, kids, you're not getting any of this when I die.' Why wouldn't I give it to my kids?

Live. Laugh. Love.

It would be different if I didn't think they had a good work ethic. In that case, I wouldn't give them a penny – but all three of them are grafters. When Shane came back from America after doing his coaching badges, the first thing he said was that he wasn't sure if he wanted to follow football as a career any more. 'OK, then,' I said. 'I'll give you a few days to get over your jet lag and then you can go and get a job.' There was no moaning or anything, although I seem to remember it taking him about two weeks to get over his jet lag! He ended up working in a bar first and then in Burton menswear. After that he got a job as a bluecoat at Pontins, which was where he learned his trade – like his dad before him.

I get loads of letters at the *Mirror* from parents whose kids are taking the piss and aren't contributing and I'm the first one to say, 'Stop doing everything for them and just kick 'em out!' Not there and then – but you know what I mean. Give those kids an ultimatum and tell them to get their arses in gear. Some of those who write to me have got kids in their late twenties or early thirties who just sit around playing PlayStation all day and their parents sound like they are literally tearing their hair out.

I know, as a parent, how hard it can be to have a conversation about life and careers with one of your kids and I actually felt quite bad having the one that I did with Shane. If I hadn't, though, I'd basically have been giving him a licence to do exactly the same as the kids I hear about in the letters I receive, and the longer you leave these conversations the harder they are to have.

132

I actually think that the majority of people who write in already know what the solution is and, by writing to me, they're just buying themselves a bit of time. You know, putting off the inevitable. I always hope that my reply will be the thing that actually pushes them to march upstairs, fling open the bedroom door and say, 'It stinks in here! Open a window, you little sod, get some clothes on and get your arse out of this house and look for a job. Otherwise, I'll set Coleen Nolan on you!'

Some of the people who write in are in such a state, though. Who wouldn't be if you had a useless lump at home? It's bad enough having a husband!

Work-life imbalance

An awful lot of people ask me how to go about achieving a successful work-life balance and as a subject to lighten the mood I think it's perfect.

Why?

Because I have absolutely no bloody idea how you go about achieving a successful work-life balance! All I know is that I'm a bit of a lazy cow and if I had to write myself an inscription for my gravestone it would be, 'Here lies Coleen Nolan, never knowingly overworked!' You just speak to my manager, Melanie, about that. She'll tell you. For a start she says that I'm the only person on her books who never answers the phone when she calls and the reason I don't answer it is because I know it'll be about work! Everyone else on her books phones *her* up asking what's going on, but not me. I just hide and hope she goes away!

In all seriousness, achieving a successful work-life balance is something I've struggled with all of my life, really, for the simple reason that my professional life has always been quite unpredictable. All I've ever been able to do is take things a day at a time and do my best. It's the original chicken-and-egg situation, really. In order to live a good life you have to work and in order to work, you have to put the effort in and make time. There's no magic formula, unfortunately, and just being aware that it's something you want to achieve will at least make you try.

The thing is, work and money have never been the most important things in my life and they never will be. Especially now. I'm almost permanently horizontal these days and it's only a matter of time before I'll have to be winched out of bed in the morning and then lowered into my chair on *Loose Women*. Joking aside, I've had to work hard to get to this point and I've also had my fair share of struggles and setbacks over the years, many of which are mentioned in this book.

One of the biggest, 'Should I, shouldn't I?' work-life quandaries I've had in terms of opportunity was when the musical *Legally Blonde* came over to the UK. The producers wanted me to play one of the lead roles without even auditioning. Career-wise, it would have been massive, but the problem I had was the length of the contract. They wanted me to sign for a minimum of a year, which would have meant either relocating to London with Ray and Ciara or only getting to spend a day a week with them at home.

I had already done the relocation thing several times before: that was never going to be an option. The thought of spending just one day a week with my family was even worse. I simply had to turn it down. I'm not saying I wasn't tempted (or, perhaps, curious) but had I gone ahead with it I know that I'd have regretted it immediately.

A lot of people would have taken the job and I completely understand that. Careers in showbusiness can disappear overnight and I can guarantee that the majority of people who are working in the industry are worried about how long their current job will last. I fully appreciated what I was turning down but, at the end of the day, it was basically just more money and I already had some of that – not loads, but enough for us all to live a good life. A year without Ciara was something I would never be able to replace and the more I thought about it the more I thought, No bloody way!

While we're on the subject of theatre, I have been tempted to give *Blood Brothers* a go, perhaps in Manchester or similar, on a short run. The thing is that four of my sisters have played the lead role over the years and every single one of them has been fabulous. I have a morbid fear that I might end up being the only shit one and I couldn't stand that. Had *they* all been shit I'd have been on that stage faster than you can say 'Luvvy, daaarling.' It's bad enough being the tallest and the youngest Nolan sister, but the shittiest?

Nevertheless, I am for the first time in my life, in a place where I am one hundred per cent happy and a lot of that has to do with the fact that I can do absolutely bugger all if I want to, either on my own or with people I love. I'm obviously very lucky to have a career that allows me space, and even during busy periods I'm fine with it. In fact, last year I was doing *Loose Women*, *At Home with the Nolans*, and *The Real Full Monty* all at the same time. I worked seven days a week for eight weeks solid, but I enjoyed every minute. Partly because I love what I do and was grateful for the work, but also because I knew that after those shows had finished filming I'd be able to relax a bit. It's either feast or famine in my line of work and, as long as there isn't too much famine, that suits me down to the ground. Send me away to hibernate for a few weeks and then drag me out when you're ready for me!

My first consideration when I'm offered work these days is, how long is it going to take me away from home? Not how much money I'll get. I shudder to think how much money I've turned down recently. I bet Melanie would be able to tell you, and to the pound, probably! I think my limit for being away from home is about two weeks. Anything more than that would just depress me. I enjoy what I do but, at the end of the day, it's just a job. That's all.

I'd never dream of telling anyone else what to do when it comes to their job but if you're in a position where you're living to work and not working to live, do yourself a favour and at least think about what you might be able to do to improve things. We only get one crack of the whip (unless you believe in reincarnation)! Even if it's just a small thing like trying to work from home once in a while or arranging a bit of me time. You won't regret it.

Bucket list, impostor syndrome and nerves

What do I still want to do? I thought a list would be a really nice way to finish off the chapter, as it doesn't involve lazy men, rubbish recording contracts or trolls! I've had to think about it long and hard though. I'm a simple woman with simple tastes and have never really been that ambitious. For anything! I want to be happy, of course, and I want those I love to be happy too. Above and beyond that? Oh, I don't know.

I did have a go at acting a couple of years ago, which I'd been meaning to do. I was offered a part in a play called *The Thunder Girls*, which was written by my manager, Melanie Blake. I'd never acted previously and had to audition first. 'You never know, I might be shit at this,' I said to Melanie. I ended up having a whale of a time and the play was a big success. I also got some really good notices (or reviews), which was a surprise. I didn't know how to take these as I didn't feel like I'd been acting. I was just being me.

I know I must sound dead boring but apart from acting, which I've done, the only thing still on my bucket list is to remain being happy. And to have an occasional shag, of course! As I said, I'm a simple girl with simple tastes. A cup of tea, a fag and an occasional shag. What more could a woman ask for? I firmly believe that there's no point in having lists of things you want to achieve – isn't it better just to be happy as you are rather than waste your life always wishing you had more?

I've got terrible impostor syndrome. This is where you doubt your own talent and skills and think that, some day, everyone is going to find out you're a fake and not responsible for your own success. I go to bed at night sometimes thinking, I wonder if that's going to happen to me? I think that's because I've never had friends in high places and have always come into a job either by the back or side door. I'm usually far too common for the people at the top and I'm also a very poor arse-licker! If I don't like you I can't go out and have dinner with you and say you're wonderful. I'll go out and say you're an arsehole, but if I do that you might not pay the bill! What I think I'm trying to say is that I'm not very good at playing the game, but do you know what? At least I can sleep at night!

I've read that impostor syndrome tends to affect women a lot more than men, which is an interesting fact. That said, the feeling does affect everyone at times, as it relates to self-esteem and self-worth and nobody is exempt from low points in those departments, particularly in my line of work. It's so easy to feel unsure of yourself and wonder when other people will realise you feel like that. My advice to anyone else in this situation would be to take a step back, evaluate things and have a word with yourself. Treat yourself like you'd treat your best friend if they were going through the same thing. I mean, what would you say if your best friend came up and said that they were suffering from impostor syndrome? You'd tell them that Mr Impostor was talking a load of bollocks, wouldn't you? You need to do exactly the same thing for yourself.

Another reason I have impostor syndrome is because, whatever I've done over the years professionally, I've never had to become another person to do it. You know what I mean – I haven't had to act. Whatever I do, I'm always being me, the opposite of what people think. It's also why I've never considered myself to be a celebrity. In whatever situation, I am, and always have been, just me.

People have many assumptions about me being famous and one of the main ones is that I suffer from nerves. People have always said to me, 'Ooh, you must get so nervous singing or being in *Loose Women*!' and, until recently, I'd always say, 'No, not really.'

What I used to experience as a singer before a concert is what you experience when you're queueing up for a roller-coaster. There's a part of you saying, 'Don't do it,' but an even bigger part saying 'Do!' and, although you might feel a bit sick up there, in the end you have a great time. But because of my battle with impostor syndrome (which I am actually winning), over the past few years my nerves have become a lot worse, to the point that if I let them, my nerves could prevent me from working. Sounds dramatic, doesn't it? It's true though. I get very nervous doing *Loose Women* and I've been doing it twenty years! I told somebody that the other day and they said that I was very good

139

at hiding it. 'That's because I'm absolutely full of bullshit,' I said to them. 'Inside, I'm dying, though!'

The kids are always really shocked at how nervous I get before *Loose Women*. Because it's shot in London they don't usually see me before we start filming. On the occasions they do, they're like, 'Wow! Are you OK, Mum? Why are you so nervous? You've been doing it a hundred years!'

Dealing with nerves is something I'm not really equipped to advise on, especially as they're getting worse as I get older! What I would say, though, is that taking a few deep breaths and having a word in your own ear can work wonders sometimes. Nerves are down to confidence usually, or a lack of it; that's what you have to work on.

I've said a dozen times in this book that you *have* to try and believe in yourself and the reason I'm repeating it so often is because it is a genuine issue. I know that you can't just flick a switch and feel confident and less nervous. If you could, I'd have a bloody great big switch to flick at home! There are things you can do though and one of the most important is becoming one of your own best friends, if that makes sense.

Remember what I said about treating yourself like you would your best friend? Give it a go.

It's a matter of life and death

Body image

Body image was very different when I was growing up. Obviously, you still had all the same teenage angst about how your body looked, etc. but what you didn't have was social media. I'm sorry to mention social media again, but there's just no escaping it!

That is the main difference though as social media has allowed people to compare themselves to everyone else. Before, if you were being compared to someone, you didn't know about it and, even if you were famous, it would only happen in the newspapers. Now it happens constantly, more's the pity.

Did I have any hang-ups about my body when I was a teenager? Of course I did! We might not have had social media but the pressure was still there. Most people I knew wanted longer legs and bigger boobs. I was with them on the legs, but last thing I wanted were bigger boobs. They've been the bane of my bloody life!

What the whole social media explosion has done, though, is basically plant anxiety in the heads of millions of people and, in that respect, it's done a lot more harm than good. I get that people want to look their best but when society dictates that, in order to be successful, popular or even happy, you have to look a certain way – which is the message we hear via social media – well, I'm afraid I find that sickening. You can't blame social media itself. After all, it's us humans who have decided to use it that way. It brings out the worst in us sometimes.

What's really daft is that, now that you have filters, nothing is real anyway! We obviously didn't have those back in the day when I was singing with my sisters. In fact, after a photoshoot you sometimes didn't see the finished article until it appeared in the magazine or newspaper! Sometimes the photographer would take a Polaroid beforehand so you could get an idea of what was coming, but even that was rare. Could you imagine somebody on Instagram taking a photo of themselves and then posting without even looking at it or applying a filter? It'd give them a bloody heart attack!

I've never really grown out of not being able to see my photos after a shoot and, if somebody asks me, I always say, 'No, thanks!' They always ask me why and I always reply, 'Because I know I'm going to be critical of myself,' which I would be. 'As long as you're happy with them,' I say, 'so am I.' They must all think I'm daft, but the last things I need are anxiety and doubt in my head. You know that some people say that knowledge is power? Well, when it comes to how I look, ignorance is bliss, as far as I'm concerned!

Fortunately, neither me nor my sisters ever suffered with any kind of hang-ups or eating disorders. There were times when I'd see a photo and think, Oh, my God, I look so fat in that! Looking back, I realise how futile that was and that I was anything but fat. I was sixteen though and that's what goes through your mind at that age. The only thing that ever made me feel self-conscious was my size compared to my sisters. By the time I joined the group, not only was I taller than all of them but I also had bigger boobs. I was like an Amazonian! It didn't really affect me as such, but I was always conscious of the difference.

When it comes to filters and touching up photos, as long as you're honest with yourself and your audience, then there's no problem. It's when you start trying to pass them off as the real thing that you make trouble for yourself. In fact, research shows that nine out of ten young women will manipulate a photo of themselves before posting it on social media because they're fearful of what people will think of the real them. How sad and scary is that?

We're doing a campaign on *Loose Women* at the moment called Body Stories, which has been designed to help promote the idea of ditching filters and accepting the real you. Each of us had our photo taken for the campaign wearing a swimsuit and the photographer then manipulated the photos and we compared the reality with the fantasy. As you might expect, there were things about the filtered photos that we all thought were marvellous – a couple of inches off the hips, etc. – but there were also things about the natural photos we loved, too. The point being that, if you start using filters on a regular basis you're liable to lose touch with and even reject the real you. It must be tempting to use them sometimes but, at the end of the day, you'll always get found out and the only person you're really fooling is yourself.

I'm no angel, by the way. I'll sit there at home reading a newspaper or a magazine and I'll go, 'Ooh, she shouldn't have worn that. It makes her look huge!' Come on, we've all done it. What I don't do, however, is broadcast my opinions and thoughts on social media. I'd never forgive myself! If you won't deliver your comment to someone's face then don't tell them via the internet!

You get all kinds of shaming, often done on social media, these days. Fat-shaming, skinny-shaming. It's awful. I know people who are naturally quite skinny who've been shamed online. Why on earth would you do that, though? I suppose it must be jealousy a lot of the time, or insecurity. Either that or the people doing it are just pathetic bullies who get a kick out of making people miserable. I honestly don't understand it. What we need to do, in my opinion, is learn to appreciate who we are, as we are. If our bodies are in working order that should be celebrated, not the fact that a bunch of people approve of what that body looks like. That said, it's probably taken me fifty years to come to that conclusion. I've thought it on many occasions, but I haven't actually believed it until recently. Not fully.

I've told this next story many times before but it's so shocking and had such an effect on me that I think it's worth repeating here. About twenty years ago, I was invited to meet a television executive to discuss a prime-time show that my agent had put me up for. I can't remember what the show was called, or even if it went ahead, but the company who were making it were interested in me fronting it, so off I went. For the first half an hour or so, the TV executive sat there, telling me how wonderful I was. 'We think you're this' and 'We think you're that.' It was all a bit sickening really. Then, completely out of the blue, he pointed at my tummy and said, 'But what are we going to do about that, Coleen? Have you considered having a gastric band?'

What makes this even more ridiculous is the fact that at the time I was a size fourteen. Had I been a size thirty-two and he was worried about my health, then I'd have understood it – but a size fourteen? The average dress size in the UK at the moment is actually sixteen but what he obviously wanted was a size eight or something.

'I beg your pardon?' I said, giving him one of my famous death stares.

'A gastric band,' he repeated. 'I wondered if you'd considered having one?'

This moron still hadn't got the fact that I wasn't very happy. It was time to let him know.

'I suppose I could lose some weight if I wanted to,' I said. 'But you're going to be stuck with that face for the rest of your bloody life!' With that I got up, shot him another death stare – the pitying kind this time – and marched out. What an absolute arsehole, I thought to myself. I should have slapped him really. Or kicked him where it hurts!

The saddest part of this story is that, a few years later, I went down to a size ten after going on a diet and doing couple of keep-fit DVDs and the amount of work I got offered afterwards was astonishing. I went from being somebody who worked quite regularly to somebody who was genuinely sought after. However, rather than making me feel better about myself, my new lease of life actually had the opposite effect. For the first time in years, I could walk into a shop, try something on and look great in it, yet I did not derive one ounce of pleasure from the experience. In fact, I felt like I'd lost a bit of me, to be honest. In weight terms, of course, I'd lost quite a lot of me, but for who?

This put me in a very difficult situation, mentally. Why? The attention I received was astonishing, but not because I looked good. It was because some people were just waiting for me to put the weight back on. It was horrible. I'd get photographed eating a burger or something and the headline the following day would be something like, COLEEN PILES ON THE POUNDS!

My sense of humour had always been very self-deprecating. Not because I lack confidence, but I just find that style funny. When I was a size ten, though, I couldn't exactly sit there on *Loose Women* and say during a discussion about dieting, 'Well I'd rather have a cake.' I realised I was pretending to be somebody I wasn't. Not just physically, but mentally. I actually didn't know who I was any more.

When I first lost the weight, my sisters would call me after an episode of *Loose Women* and say, 'My God, Coleen, you look fantastic!' Soon, as I started losing sight of myself, they were ringing to say, 'You were really quiet on the show today. What's up?' Instead of hiding it, I'd say to them that I was a bit lost, in all honesty.

What I didn't want to do at any point was say to myself, 'Sod this,' and then start regaining the weight I'd lost. It was more that I just didn't want to be so obsessed about the way I looked. You know what I mean; constantly worrying about whether or not I was pleasing people and whether or not I looked good enough to get a job. I was becoming paranoid and neurotic and that wasn't like me at all. Worst of all though, it was actually making me feel unhappy, which, if I'm not mistaken, is the opposite of what weight loss is supposed to do.

The realisation that I was doing all this for other people and not actually for me was a massive wake-up call. The people who knew, loved and cared for me didn't recognise me any more and the people who I was ultimately doing it for – who didn't give a toss – were waiting for me to fail. My priorities were arse about face, but the pressure you feel once you're on the treadmill is incredible. Every day people would be calling me up and asking what I'd eaten or whether or not I'd trained that day. At first, I used to just take it but when I realised what was happening, I stopped. When I look back at the photos from that period, I have to admit that I don't look bad at all. If only I'd felt great too!

By far my biggest weakness in the food department was snacking and nothing's really changed much there! I blame Shane Jr and Jake though. I'm sure this will resonate with a lot of people: when you have kids you stop thinking about yourself, to the point where you no longer eat three square meals a day. Or even one, for that matter! I can almost picture all the heads nodding. It's true, though, isn't it? When the boys were young I'd cook them fish fingers and chips or whatever for tea and whatever they left, I'd snaffle. I always used to set off to the bin with the leftovers but, by the time I got there, it had all gone. That happened at every meal and with snacks too. I'd give the boys a couple of biscuits each and if they left one, I'd have it. Perhaps I subliminally gave them two each hoping they might leave one? Who knows? I wouldn't put it past me! Before I knew it, though, that became a habit and the weight just piled on.

You know all these people who have a baby and then are back to being a size ten about two days later? The papers and social media are absolutely full of them these days. That's the kind of person I was pretending to be, I think, someone who just 'snapped back' and could lose weight effortlessly. I'd love to know what percentage of the people who put themselves through that are doing it for the right reasons and are genuinely happy. I bet it's quite low. Or am I just a cynical old snacker?

The really stupid thing about losing all that weight and becoming a different person was that carrying a few more pounds had never been an issue for me. It's other people who have problems with my weight and the mistake I made was listening and being influenced by them. I was persuaded – both subliminally, via advertising and watching TV, and directly, by people who were linked to me professionally – that being a size ten would make me a happier and healthier person. And I believed them! That's five years I'll never get back. I'm joking, really. It wasn't all doom and gloom during that period, but it wasn't all smiles either. Not by any stretch of the imagination.

Some of the diets I went on were ridiculous. Once again, I can imagine all the heads nodding away furiously here! We've all done it, though. The worst was a liquid-style diet. I lost three stone in three months and all I had was liquid four times a day, the equivalent of five hundred calories. I had to go and have my blood pressure checked once a week and I remember my doctor saying, 'Please, please, stop this, Coleen. It's so unhealthy!'

I didn't say as much but each time he said this, I used to think to myself, What do you mean, stop? I'm losing eight pounds a week!

When I went out for meals with my family while I was on the diet, they would all be tucking into something nice while I'd be sitting there with a glass of water. They used to play merry hell with me, saying that the contrast between what we were consuming was ridiculous!

What attracted me to this diet was obviously the speedy effect. I lost the weight quickly and the more weight I lost the more I was told how fabulous I looked. I'd tried other diets where I might lose two pounds a week and had become fed up by the slow progress. Or, at least, the lack of visible progress. I was well and truly under the spell of my liquid diet.

After three months of following the regime, I was feeling very, very weak, which is when I decided to stop. Looking back, the situation was silly. I was cooking dinner for everyone, night after night, and then sitting down with a glass of water. The trouble is, the moment I started eating again the weight just piled on. Apparently, once you come off a liquid diet, your body hangs on to everything you eat because it thinks it's going to be starved again and that's what happened. I must have put on about two stone in the first month and losing that became a real problem. It just wouldn't come off.

Soon after knocking the liquid diet on the head I met two women who'd both gone completely bald after following the same programme; they hadn't been getting the right nutrients. Then I heard about a woman in her thirties with three kids who'd had a massive heart attack and died. I dread to think what might have happened had I stuck to the strict diet.

Like most things, when it comes to weight it's about finding a balance. What makes you happy, food-wise, probably won't make you healthy and vice versa. It is possible to meet somewhere in the middle, though, without being either miserable or as big as a house. You just have to work at it, that's all.

After my second divorce I went in the opposite direction: outwards, in other words! Seriously, though, I took not giving a shit to a completely different level and I started eating everything in my path. Even the dogs weren't safe! I remember thinking to myself, I just don't care now. I really don't. I can eat whatever I bloody well like. I didn't have to make an effort for my husband any more. It was great. I loved it! It was all part of feeling free again, I suppose.

This course of action wasn't anywhere near as dangerous as losing a lot of weight so quickly, but after a couple of years of hoovering up everything in my path I had become – how can I put it – a little bit larger than I'd have liked. I was also tired all the time and quite lethargic, which was what made me want to change. I can handle carrying a few extra pounds but feeling knackered all the time's beyond crap.

What I'm not going to say in this chapter is that diets don't work. They do. In fact, every diet I've ever tried has worked, in the sense that it's helped me to lose weight. The problem is the side effects they have. I once went on a diet that made my skin break out in massive spots – which was nice! What you have to remember is that, when it comes to diets, the bigger the promises their creators make, the higher the price will be, in terms of how much it'll cost you financially, physically and, sometimes, even mentally.

Not all diets are bad for you – anything but, in many cases – but the moment you are encouraged to start cutting out food all together, you really should think twice about it. And I hate to say it, but exercise really does work. I don't like to admit it because I must have had at least ten personal trainers over the years and each one has promised me that if I keep up the exercise I'll begin to love it. Really? I don't think I've come close! Since becoming a vegan – yes, I know! I'll come on to that – I've definitely had more energy, which has helped me do more, but 'love exercise'? I don't think so.

A few years ago, my physio said five words that made me want to kiss her full on the lips. She said, 'You must not go running.' It was like winning the lottery. The thing is, although I don't exercise much in the running and jumping sense, I'm always on my feet and apart from at meal times I never sit down.

I think my point here is that you have to be honest with yourself and you have to listen to your body. If you're feeling bloated and lethargic the chances are you might need to up your exercise rate and eat more healthily and if you're feeling weak and lethargic – like I did – you probably need to do the same, just with more food! Listening to your body and acting accordingly is one of the most important things you can do for yourself and my only regret is that I didn't do it sooner.

The bloody menopause!

Me deciding to lose the weight I just talked about or, at least, some of it, coincided with the menopause. I was going to do a really big chapter on the menopause but can I be honest with you? I am fucking sick of hearing about it! In fact, my heart always drops when people bring it up.

If I know them well enough I'll say, 'Stop right there! This is a no-menopause zone!'

That said, menopause is something that needs to be talked about more openly and I do appreciate that some people suffer with it dreadfully and they're the ones I want to talk to. I get letters at the *Mirror* all the time from women who have conditions such as depression because of the menopause and, in that situation, I'll do whatever I can to help. It's the same if somebody stops me in the street or talks to me at an event. If they're going through the menopausal mill and need help then count me in. However, if you just want to talk about it as a topic of conversation or moan about having a hot flush, I'm out!

I don't remember my mum talking about the menopause and I never remember thinking, I wonder what's up with Mum today or, Why on earth is she constantly sweating? If she ever was sweating a lot, she never told me. I'm not saying that's the right way to go about things, by the way, as the thought of my mum suffering in silence is awful and I think it's good now that we can talk about these things. We need to make sure that women are educated about menopause and know what to expect, especially that they know how to recognise the less obvious symptoms. Just . . . let's not talk about it all the bloody time! Some people seem to use it as an excuse to have a moan or get attention. You're going through the flaming menopause, I always think. It's what happens!

I sometimes hear people say, 'Oh, I've had to call in sick at work because I'm on my period,' and it makes my blood boil. Really? You had to call in sick? I remember at school there was this one girl who was always going on about her period and, one day, she said to our PE teacher – who I absolutely loved, by the way – 'Miss, I can't do PE.'

'Why?' asked the teacher.

'Because I'm on my period.'

The PE teacher looked at her and said, 'So am I, but I'm doing PE all day. Now get your PE kit on and get back in here now.'

I didn't say anything but inside I was literally bursting. *Get in there*! The people who use the period as an excuse to get attention, moan or skive, are just making things more difficult for the people who actually suffer. Isn't that always the way though? Just shut up and bloody well get on with it!

You can't beat a good rant sometimes. Anyway, where was I? The menopause.

As well as feeling tired all the time because of the weight I'd put on, I also felt a bit crap generally and, although I didn't realise at the time, that was down to the menopause. My brain was telling me that nature was now done with me and it almost felt like I was redundant as a woman. I didn't entirely understand that the menopause was begin-ning, however, because I was still having periods. This is 'perimenopause', also known as menopause transition. The thing is, from the moment I started having periods I'd suffered terribly with them and, despite the menopause causing me some problems, when I finally stopped having periods it was a massive bloody relief. I must be one of the only people on Earth who's actively prayed for the meno-pause to arrive, but it's true.

The worst thing I remember happening when the actual menopause arrived was feeling for a short period of time that there was no longer a point to me being here. Not in a suicidal way. I just felt like I no longer had a purpose in life, which was actually pretty demoralising. I mean, how on earth do you process something like that? What I had to keep doing was reminding myself how preferable the menopause was to going through bloody agony every month with periods. That was hard at first and, to be brutally honest, I probably wallowed in this for a while – in the sense that, as opposed to being good to myself and helping myself to turn a corner, I fed off the sympathy and attention I was receiving. Well, it made a change from cakes I suppose!

You know the kind of thing though: 'Poor Coleen. She's going through the change.' Then one day it hit me that I couldn't change what was happening and I should really be embracing the fact that I was finally period-free! Incidentally, the only piece of advice I'd give somebody who was suffering with the menopause would be to get online as soon as you can and start researching it. There are so, so many resources available nowadays and, because everybody experiences it differently, the more you know they better chance you'll have of being able to help and take care of yourself. Also, don't be afraid to talk to your GP. It sounds obvious, but you'd be surprised by how many people who don't think that the menopause is a worthy condition. It is, so if you're suffering, get on that bloody phone!

I also lost some weight after the menopause – but not because I went on a bloody diet! I'd had my fill, if you'll pardon the pun; I always start thinking about food when the subject of diets comes up. As soon as somebody says, 'You're on a diet,' it makes me hungry and I start obsessing about food. People on diets shouldn't be obsessed about food, surely? Most are though. Then again, if people went on diets, lost weight and weren't obsessed about food, there wouldn't be any overweight people around and the diet companies would go out of business!

The reason I lost weight this time was a by-product of going vegan. Yes, you read that correctly. My name's Coleen and I am a vegan! Ciara persuaded me to watch a couple of documentaries about the beneficial effects of going vegan and I was so impressed that I decided to give it a go. I'm not one of those annoying vegans, by the way, who think that everyone should do as they do. It might sound selfish but I'm doing this for me, primarily, rather than for any moral cause and the fact that I don't have to eat animals any more is a bonus. Especially after realising how so many of them are treated on factory farms and at abattoirs etc. That's horrible.

Going vegan was far from easy, especially at first. There were so many things to consider. Once I got into the swing of things, though, it was fine, and I've been finding it easier every day. Also, if I go to somebody's house for a cuppa and they've only got cow's milk, I'll drink it. It isn't ideal, but I can't expect everybody to cater for my needs and I'm certainly not drinking black tea!

I'll tell you what, though, I absolutely hate telling people that I'm a vegan. Their initial reaction is usually, 'Oh, Christ, you're not one of *them*, are you?' I'm all right with people taking the piss out of me (in fact, I expect it!) but because some vegans are very passionate about their lifestyle, to the point of being aggressive sometimes, people tend to tar us all with the same brush. In fact, some of the men on Tinder will state on their profiles, 'Definitely no vegans!'

Just in case there is anyone reading this who is considering going vegan, treat it the same as you would menopause: do as much research as you can! It does take an awful lot off commitment and you'll have to make an awful lot of changes – obviously! From my own point of view, it's made me feel a hundred times better, both in myself and about myself, and the fact that I've also lost weight has been brilliant. Even if you don't become a vegan, which can seem a bit extreme to some people, looking to change your lifestyle, whether it be by cutting out diary, eating less meat or smoking fewer cigarettes (Coleen!), is always worth considering. I had nothing to lose and I've surprised myself that I've managed to stick with it. However, when it comes to those of us who have been struggling with our weight, I beg you to consider lifestyle rather than diet – it's the only way to make a proper, long-lasting change.

When I lost the weight after going vegan, lots of people came up to me and asked me how I'd done it. 'What diet are you on?' they all asked. The comments weren't as full on and congratulatory as they had been when I got down to a size ten, but people had obviously noticed that I was back to what you might call my 'fighting weight'.

'I haven't been on a diet,' I replied. 'I've just changed my lifestyle.'

To be fair to all the trainers and nutritionists I've worked with over the years (there must be at least a thousand!), each and every one of them also said that it wasn't a diet I needed; it was a permanent change in my lifestyle and they were right. It just took me a while to realise, but I got there in the end.

I don't want to bang on about it too much – as vegans sometimes do – but as well as looking and feeling healthier, I'm also much happier and, because I have faith in what I'm eating for a change and am not on a bloody diet, if I happen to slip up one night and have a pizza or a cake I don't beat myself up about it. Not that I've eaten much cake lately. I might have to remedy that!

The success of my new lifestyle is actually as much about making me feel that I am a woman again as it is about making me a slimmer version of one. When the changes started kicking in, I slowly began to feel relevant, as though I still had something to give. As well as that being a relief for my system it's put a bit of a spring in my step and I feel better now than I have done for a very, very long time.

There's nothing wrong in accepting help, of course, and if it hadn't been for Ciara making me sit down and watch those documentaries I might still be in the same situation. She didn't try and persuade me to take action, though. That had to come from me and me alone and I might just as easily have ended up on another diet. But I didn't.

Instead, I decided to alter my relationship with food completely and, rather than living to eat – which is what I did when I was on a diet – I now eat to live. Believe me, the effect is very different and is a much healthier one in my opinion.

Heading towards the departure lounge

'Heading towards the departure lounge' is one of my favourite phrases for describing getting older. At the end of the day, it's something we all have to try and accept and, in my opinion, a little bit of gallows humour can help to ease the situation. Some people use alcohol, I use slightly tasteless phrases!

There is a realisation, though – that usually hits you in your fifties – that death might not be that far away. And, not to put too fine a point on it, you often have it when your friends start dying. There, I've said it!

Every week I seem to hear about somebody I know, knew or used to work with, who's passed away. We need a bigger departure lounge! Hearing these sad news flashes provided me with an inspiration to think about altering things like my diet and behaviour. I know we've all got to go some time but I'm always frightened of missing out and the longer I can stay and hear the gossip, the better!

Jokes aside, the best thing you can do for yourself is be proactive about your health – if you think something is wrong, trust yourself and get it checked out! And encourage your friends to do the same.

Live. Laugh. Love.

One of the worst things about getting older, I think, apart from the aches and pains and going to the loo six times a night, is the pressure you're under to look younger, particularly in my line of work. I'm talking, of course, about plastic surgery and the like. I've had to battle against it for donkey's years and, although it hasn't always been easy, I'm proud to say that my face and body have never seen a scalpel. I begrudge that pressure to seem young. I begrudge it massively. I've come close a couple of times, but it's never happened. I could just blame social media again, like I always do but, in this case, as opposed to causing the problem, I think it's actually highlighted it. After all, people have been slapping stuff on their faces and having work done here and there to look younger for hundreds of years. Isn't that what we all want – to look young again?

When I first joined my sisters I never gave any of this a second thought. I was going to live for ever and my bum, boobs and face were going to remain pert and lovely for evermore! We were also on tour all the bloody time and that meant you never really had the time to be vain. Or, at least, not to an extent where it would make you consider having something like plastic surgery. In fact, the extent of our anti-ageing routine would have been a large tub of Pond's Cold Cream! It also kept us quite fit, all that running around, and we never had to worry about our weight. Seriously, girls, if you want to lose weight quickly, try performing on stage for two hours a night. It drops off!

If I have absolutely no time for plastic surgery, that's partly because it scares me half to death – thinking about when the procedure itself goes wrong or has devastating side effects – but also because I've been under pressure to have it since I was about forty. If there's one thing I hate more than being pressured to do a thing, it's being pressured to do a thing that involves major surgery – have you ever seen one of those programmes where they're cutting someone's face open and pulling things about? No, thanks! It's exactly the same as having to lose weight, I suppose – just slightly less reversable!

More importantly, though, my kids would be devastated if I had something done (they like me the way I am, which is nice!) and, over the years, they've all pleaded with me not to. I remember asking them once if I should have a facelift and I was surprised by their reaction. I thought they might have been OK with it, for some reason, but they couldn't have been more anti the idea. Had they all said, 'Yes,' I'm not sure what I'd have done as I'm a massive coward and I was relieved when they all said, 'No.' Actually, they didn't say, 'No,' they said, 'Don't you bloody dare, Mum!'

I've watched two of my sisters have a facelift. Maureen had hers done in 2018 when she was sixty-four and I remember being really angry both at her and at society. She'd always been naturally beautiful and when I saw her face all bandaged up after the operation I almost died. She was actually crying tears of blood after the op because she'd also had her eyes done. It was awful. I literally wanted to batter people after that, including Maureen. I kept on asking to myself, Why on earth would you let somebody carve your face up like that?

I'm all for plastic surgery when it's used for medical purposes. I'm thinking of people like poor Katie Piper, who had acid thrown in her face in an attack organised by a jealous ex-boyfriend, causing terrible burns, or maybe somebody whose life has been blighted by a condition or a traumatic incident. I know some people get breast reduction surgery if their boobs are so big that they have back pain and so on – I definitely understand that! But just to please or impress other people? At the end of the day, that's what it boils down to and that's what I have a problem with. When you look around, everybody looks the same, especially in showbiz and especially people my age – or even younger. I wonder why? Could it be because they all have the same plastic surgeon? Probably not, but they've probably had the same procedures.

It's actually one of the first questions people ask you these days. 'What have you had done, then?' What kills me is when people try and deny that they've had anything done when their lips are sticking out like a couple of strips of liver! 'Oh, really?' I say. 'You've not had anything done? Well, you certainly look good for it!' I know, of course, even as I'm having that conversation, that I could call up a fairly recent photo of that same person on Google and they'd look totally different. Anyone could see the change; the only people being fooled by plastic surgery are the people having it themselves. It's sad, really. How can you become so deluded?

It's different when someone genuinely wants a procedure for themselves – I've got all the time in the world for people who are happy to own that they've had plastic surgery. Take Dolly Parton. There's a joke I've heard about there not being a single piece of the original Dolly left now. She's all plastic! I don't think that's true, but she can't be far off. Yet, she's so self-deprecating about it and, unlike the people I've met who are totally in denial, she's more than up front about everything she's had done (quick boob joke there!) and just loves the way she looks. I remember reading an interview with Dolly in which she claimed that she sees herself like a show dog! I laughed my head off when I read that and I thought, If that's what makes you happy, you go for it! At least she's doing it for herself. She must be, otherwise why on earth would she talk about it so freely?

I wonder what started it for Dolly, though? Was it pressure she felt – having to look younger, like the latest crowd of singers, in order to sell records, or did she just like the idea of cheating the ageing process for a while and making herself feel good? I hope it's the latter, and I have a feeling it is.

People have said to me, 'Go on, just have a few little fillers. It won't do any harm. I've had them done. It'll get rid of your lines.'

'What, you mean the lines that have appeared because I've laughed a lot over the years? Piss off!' Faces tell a story and, over the past few years, I've been looking at more and more blank pages! The chances of me having even a bloody dermal filler are zero and that's because I care about what my children think and I don't care what any

TV executive or journalist would like *and* I'm happy in my own skin, thank you very much! It's taken me a long time to get to this point and I'm going to embrace it. I would encourage all women out there to do the same.

I had a major realisation about plastic surgery back in 2009. I've spoken about this before but, looking back now, I can see what an effect it had on me. I did a TV documentary called *The Truth About Beauty* in which I talked to a lot of plastic surgeons and people who'd had things done. I asked one of the plastic surgeons what he recommended I have done, if I was ever to go down that route, and – very kindly –he said, 'Well you don't need to have anything done,' to which I replied, 'That's the correct answer!' I then said, 'OK, but *if* I did, what would you do?' He then pointed out a few nips and tucks that, had I said 'Yes,' would have cost twenty grand! He'd gone from assuring me that I didn't need anything done to showing me how I could spend twenty grand quite easily. And that was just on my face!

He pointed things out that I had never noticed in my life before and, from that day on, they're the only things I see when I look in the mirror. How disturbing is that? I went from being somebody who was blissfully happy in her own skin to somebody who was paranoid about the way she looked – not permanently, but it affected me for a while.

You see what I mean about pressure? If I was in any way vain – and I'm talking about TV-vain here, as opposed to somebody who might be slightly insecure or impressionable – I'd have been hooked. That's so scary! I was forty-four years old but, by the time he'd finished pointing everything out, I felt sixty-five. I came away from that interview realising that, as opposed to making people feel better about themselves, plastic surgery – in the main – just feeds off our fears and insecurities. As realisations go, it was pretty big one, really, and although it made me feel quite uncomfortable, I'm damn glad it happened.

I'm loath to offer much in the way of advice to people who are considering having plastic surgery. What I will say, though, is make sure you're doing it for the right reasons. For you, in other words. If you're considering getting something done to make somebody else happy or make somebody else like you, take a step back and have a long old think. Is it really worth it?

For me, personally, I think the worst thing about sitting in life's departure lounge is the effect the place has had on me mentally. Over the years, I've had to have several very serious chats with myself and I don't mind admitting that, sometimes, I've found it a bit of a struggle. I suddenly became terrified of death, about the same time as I began to get the menopause. I think a lot of people experience this and, if you think about it, it's only natural. It's human instinct to survive for as long as possible and, once it actually hits you that you might be losing the battle, it can be difficult to accept. Over a few weeks, I had nightmares about dying and then, just as those were starting to fade, I began worrying about the kids. What'll happen to them when I die? I couldn't bear the thought of not being there when they needed me and the nightmares began again. It was really horrible for a time and became a kind of phobia.

Fears, worries and nightmares form a predictable human reaction to an inevitable situation and, at the end of the day, instead of worrying about dying and having nightmares, I had to start accepting my mortality or, at least, trying to. I don't know if I have succeeded in making peace with it fully, but I'm a lot better than I was. I remember speaking to Ray's mum about it a few years ago – she's now ninety-seven – and she said that she was actually ready to go. She was about eighty-five at the time and I said, 'What do you mean you're ready to go?,'

'Well,' she said. 'All old age is doing is stopping me doing the things I want to do, so I may as well not be here.'

I remember being a bit shocked by that. I just couldn't get my head around it. I shudder to think, though, of the amount of time we all spend fretting about things that we can't do anything about. Too bloody much, that's for sure!

The menopause is the same, though. In order to be able to move on from what was happening, I first had to accept the fact that my body was changing, which it was. I remember feeling quite achy when it was all going on and, once again, I had to have a word with myself. Of course I was going to have aches and pains, I told myself. Firstly, because I was getting older and, secondly, because everything was, to put it very bluntly, drying up!

There is a difference between accepting a situation and resigning yourself to it. Accepting it means moving forward and making the best of a bad job, whereas resigning yourself means lying down and letting whatever it is beat you. Bear in mind that a lot of people end up confusing the two responses. Acceptance does not mean giving up!

The other really bad thing about sitting in life's departure lounge is seeing the young people! Don't get me wrong, I adore young people most of the time – I have several living at home. They are a constant reminder, though, of what I used to have – youth – and what I used to be, which was probably not a grumpy old ratbag with large boobs, stretch marks that resemble a map of the London Underground and a bum that is on first-name terms with the back of my knees! What must it be like to be young and attractive? Remembering those days is a price worth paying, though, for having them around and one day they too will experience the same things I have. I could try and make a profound statement here, about time waiting for nobody, but I can't be arsed. We're born, we have some fun – hopefully – make some mistakes – definitely – and then we die.

Which brings me to religion. I can't not mention the R-word when talking about life's departure lounge, can I? It's also a subject I'm asked about quite a lot, which might have something to do with the fact that I'm from a large Catholic family. In this situation, people either assume I'm very much against religion or are completely devout. I think there's some truth to that in general. The people I know from large religious families tend either to have carried on the family tradition or condemned it as a load of old rubbish. Take a wild guess as to which side of the church you think Mrs Cynical here sits on?

It's really not for me I'm afraid. My mum was a very, very staunch Catholic and my eldest sister, Anne, is too. When I was a kid, I never used to say that I didn't believe in God for the simple reason that I was scared of what might happen to me if it was all true and I went to hell. I didn't actually believe in it, though. I thought of it as being like an insurance policy. You know, just in case! To be fair to my parents, they never tried to drum it into me. It might sound a bit cheesy but showbusiness was our family's religion, in that it was something we all practised and believed in.

What really finished things for me religion-wise was my mum developing Alzheimer's. Here she was, someone who didn't just go to mass once a week but had attended every single day, and I mean, *every* day. She dedicated her life to the church and you'd think, wouldn't you, that when it came to her getting older and entering life's departure lounge that God – he, she or it – might have given her an easy passing. Not a bit of it. It was bad enough that she was dying sooner than she needed to, but not being able to remember anything about the wonderful life she'd had, her family and her kids was just heart-breaking, and from a religious point of view didn't make any sense. Isn't he, she or it supposed to be loving and compassionate?

I didn't become completely *anti*-religion after that because I knew that, over the years, my mum's Catholicism had given her a great deal of comfort. In fact, I told my mum several times how much I envied her faith, for that very reason. Mum's attitude when relatives died was always, 'Well, they're going to a better place,' and I used to be so jealous of that certainty. I would lie in bed sometimes and wish I could think myself into being religious. *Please, make me believe!* I'm not sure what I was hoping would happen but, whatever was supposed to happen, it never did.

One of the most un-religious people I've ever known is my sister Bernie. In fact, she was probably more passionate about staying away from churches as my mum was about going into them! When she was dying she made it very clear that she did not want religion or faith mentioned during any part of her funeral. This actually made it quite difficult to arrange, but we got there in the end. The ceremony was held in the Grand Theatre, Blackpool, and it was more of a tribute concert than a funeral. What's more, it was absolutely fantastic and Bernie would have loved it. Originally, we were going to have a humanist ceremony but, even then, either religion or faith was going to be mentioned somewhere. Some people would probably have been OK with that, but not Bernie. In fact, I don't think I've ever met a religious person who is as passionate about their faith as she was about not having one!

I'm not quite at Bernie's level yet with regard to religion but I'm certainly moving that way. What stops me from becoming quite so vehement, I think, is the fact that I am actually open to the idea of being spiritual. I don't care about the ultimate truth of spiritualism but it genuinely interests me. Equally, it seems a lot more plausible than the stuff I've heard about and read in the Bible. What I'm trying to say, I think, is that instead of somebody telling me what to believe – based on a load of stories that are thousands of years old – I'd like to keep an open mind and decide for myself. I think the most important thing is to believe in something; I would never knock anyone for belief. It's just I like to be able to see the things I believe, in front of me – such as my family and friends.

Right, that's the R-word done. Thank God for that, eh? Or not, as the case may be!

I get a lot of letters at the *Mirror* about getting old and dying, from men as well as women. I do love my job, advising people – I'm not trying to make out that I'm Saint Coleen or anything but being in a position where you might be able to help somebody is so incredibly gratifying. And, let's face it, people need help more than ever these days. At the end of the day, though, I'm not an expert in anything and it seems to me that the people who write in obviously see me as more of a friend. Or, at least, I hope they do. Can you be an expert in getting old and dying? Well, I'm getting very good at the first, but I have no interest in trying the second. At least, not for a few years!

I don't want to sound like a stuck record but I cannot emphasise enough the importance of talking about your problems. (Except the bloody menopause! Unless you've dried up like a prune and are at death's door just keep quiet! I'm just joking.) I might not be an expert but, as well as having experienced quite a lot in life, I've come to realise that one of the most sensible pieces of advice I've ever been given is that a problem shared is a problem halved. Never has that piece of advice been more relevant than today. You have to be careful who you share it with, sometimes – remember about them being impartial – but if you get that right, you'll be more than halfway there.

I think that's another reason why people write to me, because I'm impartial. OK, so you might recognise my face, but when you write a letter or an email it's on the basis that I know nothing about your situation. It's a clean slate. One thing I have found is that, as I get older, I'm able to answer more and more letters using my own personal experiences. 'For God's sake,' I'll say. 'Don't do what I did!' There's a nice thing about getting older, actually – I am now very wise! Some of the letters I get back from people letting me know how they've got on are amazing. They really do make it all worthwhile.

Shall we try and finish this chapter with something positive? I know I keep on saying that, but I'm not sure if I've done it so far. How about the best thing about getting old? What, you mean apart from the saggy boobs, the stretch marks that resemble a map of the tube and a bum that's touching the back of your knees? Yes! Apart from all that. There must be something, surely?

Well, I've actually enjoyed all of my landmark birthdays. I loved my twenties, loved my thirties, loved my forties and I loved my fiftieth birthday. As soon as I got to fifty-one, though, I hated everything. That said, with hindsight that had far more to do with the situation I was in (splitting up with Ray at the time) than the age I was. Being fifty-one was just an excuse to have more of a moan about everything. Which I did!

I know I've probably said this elsewhere in this book but even better than the big birthdays is the fact that I do not give a shit any more, and I don't even care that I do not give a shit. I really don't! I don't mean that I don't give a shit about people any more. Of course I do still care. I just mean I don't give a shit about what the majority of people think, say or do. Deal with your own shit and leave my shit alone. That's what I say! Actually, an ability to not give a shit is probably one of the only things we older people have that young people don't these days. Well, that and elasticated waistbands!

Think about it, though; while the young are all online, worrying about how many 'likes' they've got, how they're going to cope with living for ever or how beautiful or handsome they look, we could be sitting at home in our elasticated waistbands, not giving a monkey's.

That's what we should be working towards, then: not giving a shit. How's that for a piece of advice?

What doesn't kill you

I've been through the mill a bit over the years with one thing and another (haven't we all), but I'm grateful, in a way, as each episode has made me tougher. In fact, I'm going to quote yet another popular saying here, which is, 'What doesn't kill you makes you stronger.'

Hark at me! I am literally spewing wisdom! That one's definitely true though, although some of the knocks can obviously be devastating.

The first big loss I experienced was when my sister-in-law, Linzie, died. We were both twenty-six and she and my brother Brian had just moved into their new house. I remember they had a house-warming party soon after moving in and, two weeks later, she was dead. Linzie taught aerobics and as well as doing our choreography (which I'll come to), she had just got a job in a private school, teaching dance. She had so much to live for.

When people of that age pass away, the feelings you have are obviously very different to those you experience when losing someone much older. The thing is, she also had no history of illness and it came as a complete surprise: she died of a viral heart infection, something the doctors said that she probably just breathed in. She became ill on the Tuesday, I remember, and died on the Saturday. At that time we were doing summer season in Blackpool and, because she was so good at dance, we'd asked her to be our choreographer. You remember what I said earlier – about there often being a family atmosphere during engagements like summer seasons? Well, this was that, but times ten, really, as the majority of us were actually family.

I remember we were rehearsing when Linzie fell ill. Brian rang us up on that Tuesday and said that she couldn't come in because she wasn't feeling great and on the Wednesday she was still unwell. He said she had a really bad cough and couldn't get out of bed. We just thought it was flu at that point but on the Thursday she was taken into hospital and on the Saturday she died. I think, to this day, that's the most shocking thing I've ever had to contend with and even now, as I write this, it still makes me feel very, very emotional. As well as loving each other to bits and being really good friends, Linzie and I were only a week apart age-wise. It was just awful.

Before Linzie passed away, I'd only had to deal with the death of one person in my life – my grandmother; but, to be honest, it didn't really affect me very much. It sounds awful, but she was a bit of a cantankerous old cow and I never liked going to see her. When Linzie died I experienced everything I hadn't with my grandmother – extreme shock, grief, loss, anger, confusion and fear. Every emotion you can imagine hit me like a train and, because the vast majority of these emotions were new to me, I felt overwhelmed. It remains something that I try not to bring to mind too often, for obvious reasons.

What hit me as hard as anything – and this was the same for everybody who knew Linzie – was the effect it had on Brian. Seeing somebody you love lose the person they in turn love most in the world is something you never, ever forget. We were also very close to Linzie's mum and dad and the effect it had on them was just as severe.

By far the strongest emotion I felt after Linzie's death – and also the most surprising – was guilt. A kind of survivor's guilt, I think. We were the same age, yet my mum and dad had had eight kids and would have been left with seven had I died, whereas I knew that Linzie's parents had only had two in total. It sounds ridiculous, doesn't it? At the time, however, it was anything but and when I saw Linzie's parents for the first time after she died, I was in bits. I thought that they might think her death wasn't fair and might resent us for losing her. I ended up speaking to Linzie's mum about it and she said that had never even entered her head. And why would it? But now I know that grief can have such a strange effect on how you think and all sorts of things were going through my mind.

Witnessing all that made me realise, at quite an early age, really, not only how grief can hit people differently, but also the ways in which they process and deal with it. There is no right or wrong way to deal with grief and, providing you're not hurting yourself or anybody else in the process, you should be left to get on with it. I know people who've been criticised for not wearing black or a black armband after losing somebody, which is just ludicrous. Nobody has the right to dictate how somebody grieves. It's such a private thing.

Despite Linzie dying, we were all still contracted to do the summer season and we had to just get on with it. Somebody else came in to do the choreography and, as you can imagine, the whole experience was just awful. We had to act happy, regardless of how we were feeling – the last thing we wanted to do was entertain people. It got a tiny bit easier towards the end of the run, but the first couple of weeks were probably the hardest I've ever spent on stage.

I didn't grieve for my mum until a year after she died. I obviously cried at her funeral, but that was more about the occasion itself as anything else. I was actually delighted when she died. Alzheimer's had taken her away five years earlier and, in a way, I'd already done some of my grieving. Her death was a happy release for her, I suppose. You hear that a lot in these situations. It's true, though. I mean, what's the point in being alive if you don't recognise anybody or anything and have no quality of life? Surely, it's a living hell for everyone concerned?

Usually, when a parent dies, you miss them and want them back but, because of the way Mum had been, I didn't go through that – at least, not for a good while. In fact, the last thing I was able to yearn for after she died was for Mum – as I knew her before she got ill – to return. I just couldn't imagine it. Every time I thought of her, to begin with, I pictured her with Alzheimer's. This went on for about a year until, one day, completely out of the blue, an image came into my head of me as a child with my mum. She was obviously well then and, the moment it appeared, I started crying and experienced an overwhelming desire to see her. My mind had obviously started going back, for some reason, and that's the moment I started grieving for her. It was such a big surprise and, despite the tears and the feeling in the pit of my stomach, it was actually quite a nice sensation, as it reminded me of what a wonderful person she had been.

I felt something similar when I lost Bernie. I'm not sure if it's just the way my brain works but, because we didn't see each other that often (we used to text, obviously!), after she died, I could almost pretend that she was still live, in Surrey – and that went on for ages. Could it be a subliminal form of denial? I suppose it could. Out of sight, out of mind – almost, but not in a bad way. I was probably just delaying the grief, subconsciously.

Anyway, about eighteen months after Bernie died, I was sitting at some traffic lights when, all of a sudden, I heard something on the radio that would have made her laugh. 'I better text Bernie later,' I said to myself and then went to put a reminder on my phone while the lights were still red. It only took me a split second to remember that she was no longer here but, when I did, I started sobbing immediately. I think I'd grieved to a certain extent for her, but it was only now that it hit me – I really would never see her again. I must have cried for about half an hour solid but, weirdly, after that I felt much better. I think it was a much-needed release.

Live. Laugh. Love.

When my dad was dying, my brother Tommy and I ended up in hysterics. That sounds awful, doesn't it? But we weren't being disrespectful or anything (although you may disagree when you've read this!), it was simply our way of dealing with what was happening; I've already talked about my love of having a laugh when times are tough. Half the time I laugh because I need to and half the time just because I like to laugh. At the end of the day, though, it's just another coping mechanism, really. Sometimes things are so tragic and so horrendous that they have an element of absurdity. Does that make sense?

When my dad was dying my mother got a priest in and, as Mum and the rest of us were all standing there, he started saying a few prayers. One of these prayers involved audience participation. He told us to listen until he said the name of a saint and said that at point we would all have to say, 'Pray for him.' It wasn't exactly Freddie Mercury leading his stadium audience singalong at Live Aid, but I was game.

Well, not being a churchgoer, I had no idea how many saints there are in the Catholic church but, after a full five minutes, we were still going. Unfortunately for me, the person standing next to me was Tommy and I could tell, without even looking, that he was thinking the same.

'We're going to miss the bloody funeral at this rate,' he whispered.

'I know,' I whispered back. 'He'll start to decompose!'

Well, that was it. I started getting an attack of the giggles and so did Tommy. To this day, I struggle to think of a more inappropriate place to piss yourself laughing than at your father's deathbed – and in front of a priest. Fortunately, we just managed to hold it together, but only just! Had the priest not stopped after eight thousand saints or come out with a funny one like St Felicissimus (he's a real saint), a big blue hand would have come down and Tommy and I would have been toast! (Incidentally, did you know that they have a 'saint of the day' in the Catholic church? I was just looking this up, and it's true. How very modern. Like soup of the day!)

People sometimes say, 'How can you laugh in situations like these?' It's obviously a fair question, and I have a good answer. You see, if I didn't laugh and started to cry instead, I have a horrible feeling that I wouldn't be able to stop and would get sucked into a hole. And I don't care what people think about me, I am not going to cry for the rest of my life and I am not going to let that hole swallow me up. Life and death go hand in hand and, even when somebody very dear to you dies and whether you feel like it or not, life simply has to go on. It's also my responsibility as a mother and a friend to make sure I'm in as strong a position as possible to look after myself and the people I love and if that means pissing off a few people by trying to find some-thing funny in something tragic, so be it. It's no skin off my nose.

Dad had been in a lot of pain before he died and although I missed him, his death, too, was a happy release. In truth, Dad dying was also quite a happy release for my mum, as she was able to go off and start living again. Mum was always a bit of a social animal, you see, and while Dad was happy sitting at home on an evening and watching the telly, she'd be out doing all sorts of things. She was involved with the church quite heavily, played bingo every night and she used to sing once or twice a week at a hotel. She really was a social butterfly, my mum, and she had a bigger circle of friends and a better social life than any of us. When Dad started going downhill, she had to stop all that going out and did so quite happily. When he eventually died, watching Mum get back to normal again was lovely. She had just four years before the Alzheimer's got hold of her – but they were four good years.

The perfect contrast to my mum and dad, with regard to social lives, were my sister Linda and her husband, Brian, who sadly died in 2007. Until then, they spent every minute of every day together, over twenty-nine years, and, when he died, Linda was completely lost. They really were the polar opposite to Mum and Dad. In all the years that Mum went to bingo, I don't think Dad went with her once, whereas Linda wouldn't have gone anywhere without Brian and vice versa. It's independence versus depend-ence, basically, and – despite there being no right or wrong way to run relationships and certainly no instructions – somebody who has done things independently of their partner, socially, is always going to be in a stronger posi-tion after a bereavement than somebody who hasn't.

Brian did everything for Linda and after he died she didn't have a clue. I'm talking about shopping, cleaning, cooking – the lot. She didn't even know how to bank a flaming cheque! I remember going to their local super-market after Brian had died and she had no idea where anything was. A day or two later, she rang and asked if I could come over and show her how to put the Hoover together. I felt so, so sorry for her. And it wasn't because she was lazy or anything. Anything but. They had each had a role – while Linda earned the money, Brian looked after things at home. He used to bring her breakfast in bed every morning and, by the time she got up, all the cleaning and shopping and everything had been done. We used to go, 'Jesus, Lin, where do you get me one of those?!'

I remember accompanying her to the bank once after Brian had died. She had a load of cheques to pay in and said, 'Can you go and pay them in for me?' Bearing in mind I'd already put her Hoover together by this point, I was far from keen and I almost lost my temper.

'No, I won't!' I said. 'You do it!'

'What do you mean?' she said.

'Look, Lin,' I began, 'I am not paying your cheques in for you and I think it's absolutely shocking that you don't know how to do it.'

The look on her face went from shock to fear. 'Please,' she said. 'I don't know what to do!'

'Then it's high time you learned! You just walk in, hand them the cheque with your details and then they stamp it for you.' Honestly, the way she was looking at me you'd have thought I'd asked her to kill a lorry-load of puppies. 'Get in there,' I said. 'And pay those bloody cheques in!'

About five minutes later she came skipping out of the bank like a ten-year-old. 'I've done it!' she said smiling. 'I've paid in some cheques!'

'My God, you're pathetic,' I said, grinning at her.

'But I've never needed to do it!' she said looking slightly abashed.

'I bloody know that!' I said. 'It's still shocking.'

I must admit that Linda's come on leaps and bounds over the past few years and she's hoping that by 2024 she'll be able to use the washing machine all by herself! I'm only joking. If you think about it, Linda had to learn to do in her late forties what most people learn to do in their teens or early twenties and the fact that she can now do almost all of it is a minor miracle!

I always knew that Linda had struggled after Brian's death but I found out recently that she had got seriously low. She'd written us all letters and was planning to commit suicide. This was after Bernie had died and the only reason she didn't go through with it was because she couldn't put us through what we'd already been through with Bernie. And there was me thinking she only didn't do it because she didn't know how to buy stamps for the letters!

I think Linda's biggest problem was feeling as if she no longer had a reason to get up in the morning. She didn't have kids or pets or anything. It was just her. Our mum had died a few months after Brian and, as well as having been diagnosed with breast cancer the year previously, Linda also had to undergo a single mastectomy. That was still not everything though as, just before Brian died, Linda was diagnosed with cellulitis and lymphedema in her arm. How the hell she got through all that I will never know, and I can totally understand why she was feeling like she was. Wouldn't anybody in that situation? As much as I say that I'm strong and just get on with things, had I been through what Linda had in the space of just a year, hand on heart, I don't think I'd have been able to cope. My family and friends would have prevented me from doing anything stupid I hope, but I'm not sure how I'd have been feeling mentally.

I like to think that what kept Linda alive, apart from her obvious and incredible lust for life, was her family, especially her great-nieces and nephews. She's always been a fantastic aunty and, since her nieces and nephews have started having kids of their own, she's taken things up a level. Had she decided to end it all she'd have been leaving behind seven brothers and sisters, a coach-load of nieces and nephews – who all think the absolute world of her – and a gorgeous assortment of great-nieces and nephews who she dotes on like you wouldn't believe. There's your reason to get up in the morning!

When I say that she's come on leaps and bounds over the past few years, I mean it, and that's despite what she's going through at the moment with cancer. Last year, when I started going on Tinder, I managed to persuade her and Maureen to have a go too. If I had asked a few years earlier I wouldn't have stood a chance; she wouldn't even have considered it. After Brian died, Linda suffered from a massive complex that prevented her from moving on and meeting somebody new without feeling guilty. For more than ten years, every time Linda met or even saw a man that she fancied, she'd beat herself up about it. After Bernie died, that sense of guilt went up to a completely different level. Linda felt that she shouldn't still be around.

I remember Linda saying to me after Bernie passed, 'Why didn't I go instead? I've got nothing to live for.'

I said, 'What do you mean you've got nothing to live for?'

'Bernie had a daughter and a husband,' said Linda. 'I've got nothing. I am literally waiting to die so I can go and be with Brian.' I believe now that it was around this time that Linda was considering committing suicide – not that any of us had any idea. It wasn't just a case of Linda feeling sorry for herself. She genuinely hated the fact that Bernie had died and she hadn't. I think that's probably quite a common thing for the bereaved – feeling like they can't move on and feeling guilty for surviving, but I'm so glad she got over it. She's such a warrior, is our Linda.

A lot of letters I receive at the *Mirror* are from people who are struggling to come to terms with either the imminent death or death of somebody they love and those letters are some of the most difficult ones for me to answer. I'll come to some advice in a second, but let me give you a personal experience first.

Usually, when somebody dies, whoever's lost that person will be inundated with offers of help – at first. Then, once the funeral's over, everybody goes back to normal life and that person's left on their own. I remember that's what happened to me when Bernie died. The day after her amazing funeral in Blackpool, everybody went their separate ways and the feeling of having everybody around me one minute and then not the next, was awful.

I deal with grief in the same sort of way that my mum used to. I have a good cry, get it out of my system and then just get on with it. But I think some people feel that, by returning to normal life, you're somehow abandoning or forgetting about the person you've lost. You're obviously not, but that's how it can feel like sometimes. I probably felt a smidgen of that when Bernie died but, in the main, I wanted to just get on with life as best I could.

Not only had Bernie planned every detail of her funeral, but she also left instructions for the mourning period too! 'I'll give you two weeks to cry,' she said. 'And you'd better fucking cry a lot, because I deserve it! After that, I don't want you to cry any more. I want you to get on with being alive, OK?'

To this day, every time I have a moment when I feel sorry for myself, I always think of Bernie. She was so, so strong and would not tolerate self-pity under any circumstances, and certainly not when she was ill. When somebody you love is dying, all you want to do sometimes is break down and tell them how much you love them and how much you're going to miss them. If somebody's OK with you doing that, then fine, but if I'd done it in front of Bernie she'd have given me a right bollocking.

'Just pull yourself together and go back to work,' she'd have said.

I'm not saying I didn't cry in front of her when she was ill or dying. Of course I bloody did. I'm not made of wood! There were no breakdowns though.

At the risk of repeating myself, there really is no right or wrong way to deal with the grief of somebody dying or somebody who's died and I cannot emphasise enough the need for you to just do whatever feels right and – most importantly – whatever gets you through. As hard as it might be to accept, if somebody is dying or has died there's bugger all you can do about it and your responsibility, first and foremost, is to take care of and be kind to yourself. You might think there are other people who are more deserving of your attention and care, but how on earth are you going to help them if you're being torn to pieces? You can't look after other people if you aren't looking after yourself. That's a fact.

Some of the saddest letters I get are from people who are experiencing bereavement for the first time and can't understand why they're not crying. As well as being confusing, this experience can lead to a sense of self-loathing. The biggest battle for someone like me is trying to persuade such a person to reach out to somebody and talk about it. Linda has had counselling for the past twelve years now and she'll probably have it for the rest of her life. People can see this as a weakness, though – but it's just not!

The fact that these people are writing to me means that they want to talk to someone but sometimes they simply don't know who to or how. Please, if you're experiencing grief of any kind, whether it be due to a bereavement or a breakup, then just speak to somebody. Just as importantly, though – and, yes, I know we're getting back to stuck record territory – there is no right or wrong way to express grief and if you're not bawling your eyes out every five minutes it will *not* be because you don't care. Look at me. I laugh every time I experience grief and end up insulting priests!

When I had counselling after splitting with Shane the therapist said that, in many ways, a breakup is worse than a bereavement: the person you've lost is still there. This can obviously make closure more challenging and you've got two choices in my opinion. Either bump them off or move to a different country. Easy!

One thing I do say to people, when I'm not encouraging them to murder their ex-partners, is that it's OK to have the odd day when you feel sorry for yourself. Every year, on Brian's birthday, Linda has a duvet day which she'll spend having a good blub and watching sad films, and that's fine! Wallowing days are great. Wallowing weeks and months, however, are not! If I was in that situation I'd make sure I had a wallow day every so often, just to get it out of my system! As it is I have about a dozen bloody animals to look after and the only thing I can wallow in at the moment is cat, dog and goat poo!

The next day, even if I wanted to have a second wallow day, I would force myself to get my arse out of bed. Partly because there'd be things to do, but also because I'd owe it to myself and to the person I've lost to carry on living the best life I possibly can. I'm also a nosy cow and I'd be in danger of missing something. Let's not forget that!

Live. Laugh. Love.

Being serious for a second – if you're being put through the mill with grief and you genuinely can't think of anyone you feel comfortable speaking to, try your GP. They'll be able to put you in touch with a grief counsellor who *will* be able to help you. I know it sounds obvious, but you'd be surprised by the number of people in this situation who never even consider talking to their GP. That's what they're there for! Or you could try and find a bereavement charity or a local grief support group.

Equally, if you just want some company but don't want to say anything, that's fine, too. The process of grieving doesn't always have to involve talking. The reason I encourage talking so much is because I know how helpful it can be and have met so many people who have benefited. Once again, though, whatever gets you through!

Lastly, never underestimate the healing power of time when it comes to grief. I speak to so many people who tell me that, in getting to the end of a day without breaking down or sobbing, they have a little bit more confidence and this makes them a little bit stronger going into the next day.

It does get easier, believe me. Do yourself a favour and, as part of taking care of yourself, try and treat getting through each day as an achievement.

Mistakes (I've made a few) and faults (I have none)

Big ones, small ones, stupid ones, embarrassing ones. We've all made mistakes, haven't we? That'll never change, as long as we're still alive. The best thing you can do when you make a mistake is learn from it, move on and don't have any regrets.

I think I've already said that I rarely have regrets and I also try not to look back on things too much. If you do, all you get are a load of what-ifs and that's not healthy. In fact, if I could go back and do it all again, I can't think of one major thing I'd change really. I'd still marry Shane and Ray and I'd still make the same mistakes, for the simple reason that they've helped to make me who I am, and I don't mind who I am.

Also, each mistake I've made over the years has taken me down a different path and sometimes that's been quite exciting. I'm certainly not advocating that you go out and make a load of cock-ups on the off-chance that it might be quite exhilarating, but you know what they say – one door closes and another opens, and sometimes it's worked in my favour.

Live. Laugh. Love.

What's different is making a mistake that hurts or upsets somebody. If that's the case it's fine to look back, because it's never too late to say you're sorry. I don't care if it's ten or twenty years down the line. If you're sorry about something, go and tell the person. Then you can move on. I've been on the receiving end of a hurtful mistake several times and, in the case of each, I'm still waiting for an apology! The thing is, the longer you leave it, the harder it is to do. I get that. So bloody well do it, then!

The majority of my mistakes are down to me being too trusting. I've been let down so many times by people I've trusted it's unreal. But the thing is, if I could become less trusting, I wouldn't do so. I've lost count of the number of times I've said to myself, 'Right then, Coleen, that's it! I will never trust anyone again as long as I live!'

I always do trust again, though, and if I ever made good on that resolution to be less trusting I know for a fact that I'd end up being a very bitter person, and that actually frightens me a lot more than being let down. It's obviously not an exact science, but you get my drift. Taking the chance of being let down by somebody or being bitter for the rest of your life? I know which one I'd choose – and I have!

It won't surprise you to learn that being let down can happen quite a lot in the entertainment industry and you have to take most things with a ginormous pinch of salt, especially promises. It doesn't mean you can't trust anybody in my line of work, but you have to be prepared for disappointments along the way and you have to have – or, at least, try and develop – a very thick skin.

Mistakes (I've made a few) and faults (I have none)

One of the steepest learning curves I had in this respect was when I was sacked from *This Morning*. The number of promises that were made to me during that period was ridiculous and ninety-nine per cent of them meant absolutely nothing. Instead of allowing that disappointment to turn me cynical and bitter, however, I decided to just be wary going forward and bear in mind that the industry I work in can be very false. It isn't always, but it can be.

Something else I'm definitely guilty of is being too much of a people-pleaser. My son, Jake, is always telling me off and it's something I battle with. The fact is, though, I just want everyone to like me! Not because I've got a massive ego, but because I don't like being despised or slagged off. I know loads of people in the business who couldn't give a shit what the public think of them but, unfortunately, I always take it personally. I'm definitely better than I used to be though. Twenty years ago it was the bane of my bloody life and barely a week went by without me lying in bed all night, worrying, because I'd been slagged off by some idiot in the papers for wearing the wrong colour dress!

Even now, when people say nasty things about me on social media, all I want to do is get them all in a room and say, 'Why do you all hate me? I promise you I'm nice! Please like me!' Some people genuinely can't stand me, though, and they're not scared of telling me either. I always think, You don't have to tweet that you think I'm an arsehole. I was living in ignorant bliss until that point. Keep it to yourself! Or, if you must, just tell your friends.

Live. Laugh. Love.

When I began listing my faults, I thought it was just going to be me being too trusting and being too much of a people-pleaser, but now I'm actually writing this chapter they're coming thick and fast!

Number three on the list is suffering from guilt unnecessarily. Or, to be more precise, Irish-Catholic guilt! I know I'm not a practising Catholic but I'm pretty sure the guilt was being drummed in from the day I was born and has stayed with me ever since. Or, at least, some of it has. It can manifest itself in lots of different ways but probably the most annoying trait is putting other people first, to a ridiculous degree. It drives my kids insane and I do it with everything. If we get a takeaway and the cooks get the order wrong and one of the kids is missing their dish, I'll always say, 'It's OK. You have mine. Honestly, I'm not hungry.' Even if I am hungry, I'll insist that they have my food and if they don't, I'll feel incredibly guilty. It's not just that, though – I suppose, in reality, it's a cross between guilt and wanting to look after the people I love. Either way, it can be a massive pain in the arse if you're on the receiving end, as I'm often told!

Kids are clever though, aren't they? Mine have started turning this characteristic I have on its head and, if we're all trying to make a decision about something, which would normally end in me saying, 'I'll do whatever you lot are happy doing,' they'll say, 'We want to know what *you* want to do, Mum,' and they won't take 'No' for an answer. To be honest, I can't stand this retaliation, as it goes against everything my mind is telling me – which is to just do what

194

everyone else wants to do and make my kids happy. I actually annoy myself sometimes!

It's not a martyr thing, by the way. I don't sit there thinking, Aren't I great? I just gave you my food, or, I've let you take my car for two days and now I've no car. I just have this urge to put other people first and live by the philosophy that if they're all right, I'm all right.

I'd love to know how many of you reading this do the same thing. I bet there's loads of you, particularly other mums. It's something I don't think I'm ever going to be able to change. The behaviour is far too engrained and the effect I feel when I do give something up for my kids is irresistible. In fact, I'd say that's when I'm at my happiest. If I was treating myself to something while they were struggling with an issue – even if that was something completely unrelated – I'd still feel horribly guilty. It's funny how the mind works. Well, it's funny how *mine* works!

The only way you can change your habit of always putting others before you is by valuing yourself. That's the starting point. I'm certainly not perfect in this department myself, but if the attitude of my kids was just 'Take, take, take', then it would be no effort to act the opposite way because, as much as I love my kids, I do not suffer fools gladly and refuse to be a mug. If I think somebody's treating me badly or being unfair I'll say so. What's more, I'll be very pissed off!

We're back to marriage again; the first time I realised to any great degree that I always put others first was when I was with Ray. I let that be a part of our relationship for years. Do I regret that? A tiny bit, I suppose. By far the stronger emotion I feel, however, is gratitude; once I came around to what was happening I changed the way I was thinking and started to value myself more. If Ray had done the same, we might still have been together, but he was far too set in his ways for that.

Sometimes you just have to sit down and ask yourself, What do I want and why am I the one who's always trying to please everybody? It took me five years to ask myself that question. I'd convinced myself that I was happy because Ray was happy, but I wasn't at all, because he wasn't trying to make me happy. I know loads of people who have convinced themselves that as long as their other half and kids are happy they are, yet they get treated like shit. If you're in that situation, please ask yourself, What do *I* want and why am *I* the one who's always trying to make everybody happy?

When I asked that question, my thought processes changed completely. It wasn't as if I suddenly wanted to be showered with roses or have people telling me how wonderful I was (although it would have been nice!), but it did make me realise how much I was being taken for granted and it was quite a shock, to be honest. Imagine if I had done that after twenty or thirty years! The word 'change' is easy to say but not always easy to do. You have to try, though.

I have so many people write to me who just don't believe in themselves. You remember I said I wanted people on social media to like me? The point is that, even if they don't, it doesn't stop me from liking me. It just makes me think, Why don't you like me, because I think I'm really great! Let's discuss why you don't like me and then decide that you do! (That's a joke, by the way!) What stops all that hateful troll bollocks from genuinely affecting me is that I do have a certain amount of self-esteem.

Second only to hating people for no apparent reason, the thing that both baffles and upsets me most in life – and again, it's rife in the entertainment industry – is people being unjust. The best example I have to offer is the whole Kim Woodburn thing, which affects me to this day and remains one of the most emotionally damaging experiences I've ever had to endure. In fact, other than losing family, that's probably been the lowest point of my life. It was horrendous. I was, basically, abandoned by one or two people – and these were figures I thought would have supported me – over something I didn't do. As with every other challenge in my life, I did eventually manage to learn from the experience and take something positive away, but the damage it did has far outweighed any benefits.

Just to refresh your memory, in 2018 I was accused of bullying Kim Woodburn after she came on *Loose Women*. The two of us had clashed on *Celebrity Big Brother* several times and the idea of Kim appearing on *Loose Women*, I was informed, was to try and clear the air. Knowing how Kim had behaved in the Big Brother house I was sceptical, but I was willing to give it a go . . . eventually.

Sure enough, as opposed to being in any way concilia-tory, Kim came on wanting a fight but, rather than allowing her to steamroller everyone as she'd done on *Big Brother*, I gave as good as I got. I still don't know why, but some viewers decided that I was bullying Kim – this was rubbish – and, thanks to certain people and certain circumstances, rather than the accusations being dismissed as they should have been, they were taken as gospel by the press and by people on social media. A witch hunt began. A witch hunt that made me want to give up showbusiness for ever.

Everyone experiences criticism for one reason or another but, if it's unjust, it can really hurt. The accusations around Kim themselves were most definitely unjust and what hurt even more was the number of people I knew who were happy to jump on the 'Coleen is a bully' bandwagon. You certainly get to know who your friends are in a situation like that!

What followed in the days after that episode of *Loose Women* can only be described as a campaign of hatred. I had a forty-date tour booked at the time – my first-ever as a solo performer – that was starting imminently. My manager, Melanie, had put a lot of her own money into the shows. I remember sitting in a hotel room and Melanie rang.

'Do you want to go home?' she asked. She knows me so, so well, does Melanie, and that's exactly what I wanted to do.

'Yes, please,' I said. That was Melanie for you – most managers would have made me go through with the tour, regardless. You know the old saying: any publicity is good publicity! In this case I would have been like a lamb to the slaughter. We had a massive PR campaign booked for the tour and she cancelled everything. She lost a fortune.

Melanie is probably one of the strongest people I know but when we next met up in person, she cried – it was the first time I'd seen her do this in fifteen years. She said, 'I don't know how to fight this for you because you haven't done anything wrong. I just don't know what we're fighting.'

I'm often asked why I think the witch hunt started and I always say that it's because of the way social media works. It's like Chinese whispers. A lot of people were commenting on the incident yet, when I asked any of them if they'd actually seen the episode, they'd say, 'No, but my friend has, though.' Unfortunately, the whispering just grew and grew and grew – the people who did watch the show ended up analysing and twisting every word that had come out of my mouth. Not every word that came out of Kim's mouth, though. She was being portrayed as a victim, which I didn't think was fair.

To try to put my side of the story across I ended up going on *This Morning* with Phillip and Holly and, within minutes, I broke down and started crying. I had promised myself that I wouldn't but, looking back, it was probably inevitable. I tried saying that I'd never meant to hurt anybody, which I hadn't, and – if I had – that was never my intention, which was the truth.

Within minutes of my appearance on *This Morning*, the Mail Online website had published a story under the headline, COLEEN APOLOGISES FOR BULLYING KIM WOODBURN, and so the whole damn thing kicked off again. But I had never once apologised, for the simple reason that there was nothing to apologise for! I ended up watching that episode of *Loose Women* again and again and again, just to see if I'd missed something – anything – that could help me understand why I was being vilified. I couldn't, though, which actually made it worse.

The sad irony is that the two things I hate most in the world are thieves and bullies, and the fact that I was being accused of being a bully made me feel as if I'd murdered somebody.

When I got home after having appeared on *This Morning*, the boys started rowing about what had happened and, in turn, that made me cry like a baby. 'It's affecting us all,' I said to Ciara, into whose arms I was sobbing at the time. That was really the lowest point I can remember, ever.

After blubbing my eyes out and catastrophising for a few hours, I made the decision to pull myself together and start fighting to get myself out of this situation. It was going to be easier said than done though. Some idiots on Twitter (where else?) had started a petition to get me sacked from ITV and it had received over 25,000 signatures. (Incidentally, there was a counter-petition calling for me to be kept on by ITV that I've only recently discovered – it received a grand total of forty-one signatures. Thanks, everyone!)

The trouble was that, instead of everyone in the industry backing me – which I would obviously have expected and been grateful for – some remained silent. There were people who defended me, but some didn't and, without everyone involved in the show putting on a united front, I was always going to have a battle on my hands to turn things around. What they actually said to me was, 'Why don't you have a week off and then come back?' I thought, Are you all mental? At that moment in time, I had no intention whatsoever of appearing on any television programme ever again. I was done with it. That wasn't specifically a reaction to this particular situation, by the way. I'd thought it through and had decided that I was done with showbusiness. Because, at the end of the day, in my eyes at least, it felt like showbusiness was done with me.

Over the next few days, people kept phoning and texting and, for the first time ever, instead of taking their calls or messaging them back, I put them on to Melanie. I just couldn't talk to them.

Incidentally, I'd held out on the show with Kim Woodburn for some five weeks before finally caving in. I'd wanted to keep saying 'No' because I knew what she was like and knew what would happen. But I must say that even I didn't predict the level of chaos that followed. You live and learn!

Many of the *Loose Women* panellists were absolutely brilliant, by the way, and either messaged or called me every single day. That was one of the only bright spots during the whole debacle. Janet Street-Porter, in particular, bent over backwards to defend me. She even wrote a big piece in the *Mail* at a time when I was public enemy number one and almost undefendable. It was a very brave gesture, as she could easily have lost her job. She knows me very well as a person and knew that I was being portrayed unfairly and that was why she did what she did. She's as hard as bloody nails is Janet. Like me, she doesn't like people being treated unjustly.

The number of requests I received to do an exclusive interview was incredible and if you added up how much money the media seemed prepared to put up, you could have cleared the national debt! In the end, I came to the conclusion that I just couldn't trust the press and I decided that whichever newspaper I went with wouldn't be able to resist twisting my words in some way. I declined all of them.

I still get flack about that episode. Just recently I received a direct message in my Instagram account, saying that I should be ashamed of myself because I bullied Kim Woodburn, or words to that effect. I'd often laugh at such comments and, if I could ever be arsed to reply, I always said, 'Come on, now. It was three bloody years ago. Move on!' But I have realised that it's not worth engaging with them at all. These days I just block such messages as, however confident, unaffected or vindicated you might feel, you should never engage with a troll. Unless you're throwing them under a bridge, of course!

For the first two months following the fateful show, I was adamant that I wouldn't go back to *Loose Women*. After about three months, I had a change of heart. Leaving showbusiness for ever was as good as admitting guilt and, more importantly, why the hell should I allow a lie to destroy a career that by then had endured over fifty years? It would have been game, set and match to the trolls, the press and the people who left me high and dry. I kept on repeating to myself while I was making this decision, 'You didn't do anything wrong, Coleen. Why the fucking hell should you have to crawl under a stone and disappear?' I owed it to myself to go back to the show and it's one of the most empowering things I've ever done.

The only condition I attached to returning to *Loose Women* was that the episode was never mentioned again, and it never has been. They were probably hoping I'd give them an exclusive, but I'm afraid not. In fact, this part of the book is my exclusive!

What I learned from the experience – although I don't necessarily like this lesson – is that fame will always result in people gunning for you, people who can't stand your guts, and the sooner you accept that, the better. The thing to remember – and this goes for anybody who has a problem with people not liking them – is that you should concentrate on the people who matter and forget about the ones who don't.

I'd resigned myself to being hated for a spell, but, by accepting what had happened and moving on, I was basically sticking two fingers up and telling them all to fuck off. Metaphorically, of course. Remember what I said: never engage with a troll! The thing is, we live in one of the only countries in the world where you can go from hero to zero in a matter of hours and you really do need to have your wits about you. Otherwise . . .

The other thing I took from what happened, apart from a weakened heart and some shot nerves, was a determination not to try and please everybody. I had given into the *Loose Women* crew and agreed to do the show because I didn't want to appear difficult but, in doing so, I put myself and my kids – who were also attacked via social media – through absolute hell.

Actually, now I think about it, I've got one big regret for you, after all. I knew we'd find one eventually! What I regret is not sticking to my guns when I knew, deep down, that doing the show would cause me nothing but bother. Yet I kept on asking myself whether or not I was being difficult by saying 'No,' and eventually my doubts got the better of me. What if I lose my job by saying 'No'? I thought to myself. Now when they ask me to do things, if I have even the smallest of doubts, I'll say, 'I'm sorry but I don't want to do that.' You know what they say – once bitten, twice crapping your bloody knickers!

We're back to the dangers of doing something for somebody else's benefit – whether it be looking a certain way or doing a certain thing. The question you always have to ask yourself in such a situation – apart from, 'What the bloody hell am I doing?' – is whether that thing fits with your needs, your wants and your principles. You might think to yourself, Well, if it doesn't, what's the worst that could happen? You could end up bawling your eyes out on *This Morning* and making a massive tit of yourself, that's what!

Surviving motherhood
(with or without pain relief!)

I think I was born broody. Actually, allow me to rephrase that. As long as I can remember, I have wanted to have kids. In fact, it was probably my first-ever ambition. At primary school I talked to my friends about having kids and I always wanted ten. Mum had eight and I wanted to beat her by two. And the thing is, had I met the right man – i.e. not Shane or Ray – I probably would have had ten children. It's a bit of a bold statement, I suppose, but I genuinely think I would.

I was so obsessed about having babies that I used to ask my mum what it was like to give birth. Having had eight of them, I believed, there weren't many people more qualified to tell me than her, but she was never interested. 'You'll find out one day,' she used to say. I carried on asking her until I actually had one of my own but she never relented. 'You don't need to hear about my experiences. You'll be having your own soon.' Thanks, Mum! Looking back, I wish she had given me more advice, for the simple reason that she was so incredibly wise and experienced. Perhaps if I'd pushed it, she would have. Who knows?

Live. Laugh. Love.

Recently, me, Ciara and Maddy, Shane's fiancée, spent an entire day talking about birth. They're obsessed with the programme *One Born Every Minute* and they wanted chapter and verse about what it was like giving birth. Unlike my mum – who had her own reasons for deciding not to talk – I was happy to give them the full nine yards and it was a lovely day. Ciara kept going, 'No, I'm not doing it. I won't be able to,' and I kept saying, 'Don't worry, kid, you'll be fine. Just make sure you have a fucking epidural!' The only options she was considering were adoption or birth by caesarean section!

I know I've only experienced the whole process three times, but I loved being pregnant and I loved giving birth. The first one's always the most nerve- wracking or, at least, it was for me and, by the time you get to the third – if you're daft enough to have three kids – it's a doddle! As with most things I've talked about in terms of offering advice, you have to use your resources in the situation: surround yourself with as many people who can help as possible. Hopefully, some of them will stick around after the birth, as that's when the fun really starts. I loved my kids as babies but, after that, they just got on my tits! Seriously, as soon as they started moving I thought, Aww no, you're not cute now, you're just annoying!

Shall I tell you about the first time I found out I was pregnant? At the time I was so happy that I couldn't care less what anyone else thought but, looking back, I guess it was slightly stressful. I was twenty-three years old and had been with Shane for about two years. I was also the youngest Nolan Sister and, because of our squeaky-clean image, the majority of the country thought we were born-again virgins. Worst of all, Shane and I weren't married! The thought of the youngest Nolan Sister having a relationship with a man was bad enough, but getting knocked up by one *and* before they were married? It's a wonder there wasn't a series of heart attacks. Maybe there was?

In all seriousness, though, I was the first one of the sisters to have a child out of wedlock and the reaction from the press was what you might call 'mixed'. Luckily, I was far too happy to care what the press or the public thought and it all went over my head, really. The only people I was worried about telling were my mum and dad. They were from a more traditional generation and Mum was, as I've told you, a staunch Catholic. I was obviously quite worried, but it turned out I needn't have been. Both were absolutely over the moon or, at least, they said they were. I have a feeling that, although pleased, Mum was probably compromised slightly by her religious beliefs, but she never said as much. That's something I'll always be grateful for. Dad's reaction was, 'If you're happy, Coleen, that's all I care about!' It was such a nice surprise.

The pregnancy itself was just a doddle, to be honest. There'll be people reading this thinking, Whaaat? You're joking, aren't you? It's true, though. Before either of us ever got pregnant, Maureen and me used to suffer from really bad morning sickness – we were often just sick in the morning, for no apparent reason. I had no idea why at the time, it just used to happen. Then, when I actually was pregnant, I never once felt ill. How strange is that? I later found out that the sickness that Maureen and I had was caused by some kind of hormonal imbalance. My pregnancy reversed the imbalance and stopped me becoming sick!

I should have my own TV show, just because of that, really, shouldn't I?

Even if I had been sick, I'd still have loved being pregnant. I loved the way my body changed and I loved the way it felt, especially when the baby started kicking. I was absolutely over the moon when that happened. I felt really special, to be honest, like I was the first person ever to become pregnant.

The only bad thing about the birth itself was my mum's reaction to seeing me in so much pain. She was there for the whole thing and I think it hurt her emotionally a lot more than it hurt me physically. I went through the mill a bit, it's true, but she was so upset. 'I wish I could do it for you,' she kept saying, tears running down her eyes.

'Fucking hell, Mother,' I remember gasping to her. 'So do I!'

If Ciara asked me to be with her in the delivery room for her caesarean section I'd be in there like a shot. I often think that it would be better for births in general if the mum's mum was usually present instead of the baby's dad, but each to their own. I always have this vision, you see, of the dads being sent away before it starts and then, the next time he sees you, you're sitting up in bed holding your new baby. Having him standing there like a lemon throughout labour while you're shitting yourself and turning your stomach inside out seems a bit pointless to me.

I wanted to punch Shane and Ray in their bloody faces during my three births. I tolerated them at first but, after a while, they just started getting on my tits. I remember Shane saying something like, 'Go on, love, keep pushing,' and I said to him, 'Will you just fuck off!' He didn't though. He just stood there like a spare prick at a wedding. Let's face it, husbands and partners can be a pain in the arse at the best of times, but in a situation like that? Useless.

I found out, after giving birth to Shane Jr, that not only had my mum given birth eight times, but she'd also done it without painkillers, stitches or gas and air. She'd had nothing. Nothing except pain, that is! She also had to get the bus to the hospital when she went into labour because she couldn't drive and my dad was at work. It was also the time when men weren't encouraged to come to the hospital and, apart from the actual deed itself, she did everything on her own. When she went into labour she'd phone him at work and say, 'Right then, Tommy, I'm in labour. I'm off to get the bus to hospital.' 'All right, love. See you later. Good luck!'

When you arrived at the hospital in those days you were literally shown your bed and told to get on with it. My God, how times have changed! I don't think people were braver back then. They just didn't have a choice, did they? Had I been in the same situation I'd have had to get on with it as best I could.

Live. Laugh. Love.

I think Linda was the heaviest of us sisters when she was born. She was a month early and weighed about eight pounds. Thank God she didn't go full term, then. She'd have been ten or eleven pounds! Imagine giving birth to an eleven-pound baby without pain relief and no stitches afterwards. It doesn't bear thinking about. No, it really doesn't!

Shane Jr was ten days late and the midwife reckoned I'd frozen him inside me after stuffing myself with ice-cream for nine months. I've always been a big fan of ice-cream so, to actually get a craving for it – which, when you're pregnant, is basically a licence to eat – was like a dream come true. He must have been happy in there because I went into labour on the Wednesday and he didn't arrive until the Friday. To be honest, I think I was probably as reluctant as he seemed to be about the pregnancy coming to an end as, once he arrived, bang went my licence to eat! Or, at least, to eat half a ton of ice-cream every day. Nothing's at all changed in either department, by the way. I'm still addicted to ice-cream and I'd still have another baby if I could.

The difference between having Shane Jr and having Ciara, twelve years later, was immense, especially in the way I handled it. With Shane everything was so new and I was carried along by my naivety and inexperience. I remember during the early contractions thinking, Wow, this hurts! At least it can't get any worse. Except it did get worse. A lot worse! Not to the point where it bothered me that much; it was all part of the experience and I was just so happy being there. In fact, you could say that excitement at being in labour acted as a kind of natural painkiller. I told you I was a bit strange! By the time Ciara came along, I was an old hand and just sailed through. Her birth was fantastic. It was the first time I'd had an epidural (I just had gas and air and pethidine with Shane and Jake) and I felt everything except the pain! I remember feeling her actually coming down to make her appearance. I was chatting to Ray at the time and I thought, Here she comes! I even fell asleep for half an hour during the hardest contractions and Ray went off to get something to eat. The midwife woke me up very gently to ask me to start pushing. The next thing I knew, they were putting Ciara in my arms. It was all very, very civilised, actually!

Despite everything you might learn or hear before giving birth, there are certain things that they cannot teach you and cannot prepare you for. Especially the moment they put the baby into your arms for the first time. If you've never actually been in that situation, I promise you that not all of the things they don't prepare you for are horrible! They can be overwhelming though.

My first two births were on opposite sides of the scale. The moment they put Shane Jr into my arms, I felt an incredible sense of love which was stronger than anything I'd felt previously. This was followed very quickly by a horrible sense of dread, which was basically the start of what has become a lifetime of worry. Anybody who has given birth will know exactly what I mean. It's wonderful becoming a mother and, as I said, the love you feel for your newborn child is so, so special. The upshot of that love is that you don't want anything bad to happen to your child and, because the love you feel is so incredibly strong, the worries and anxieties that follow are equally intense. When Jake came along, I was obviously more confident and, although I experienced the extreme love, I had far less of the worry.

When I came home with Shane Jr things got even worse. I automatically related every piece of bad news I watched on TV to him. Seriously, the news became my nemesis! This quickly pushed me into a constant state of anxiety and I catastrophised about everything. If Shane coughed once I'd convince myself that he had whooping cough or bronchitis. I was a nervous wreck! Shane was an Olympic-standard crier who seemed to have an allergic reaction to sleep and, after a few days, I was at my wits' end. Eventually, I rang my mum and dad who came straight to the rescue. 'You're never too old to call your mum and dad' is my motto!

Later, I did rebel against my mum once or twice, when she started suggesting things like rubbing brandy onto Shane Jr's gums when he was teething. 'We've got Calpol now, Mum!' I snapped. A lot of what she suggested did work though, to be fair, but when it's your baby you want to do it your way.

My family had all moved back to Blackpool by this time and I actually felt quite isolated. I know a lot of new mums feel the same – it's all so new and overwhelming. And, of course, your hormones are all over the place and your body is still recovering from the trauma of birth. It always feels like you're the only woman to have experienced this. To any new mums feeling the same way, I'd say not to be afraid to tell somebody that you're not coping as well as you might be. There's no shame in it and it doesn't make you a bad parent. In fact, it makes you a good parent; if you didn't say anything, the situation would get worse. Just ask for help!

I felt a bit like that because I hated breastfeeding. Or, should I say, I was made to feel a bit like that. Not getting on with breastfeeding is almost a crime in some people's eyes and the number of times I had to stop myself from punching people or telling them to fuck off (I was very hormonal at the time) was ridiculous. Just remember, if you're doing your best, you're doing brilliantly and if your brilliance needs a bit of a helping hand sometimes, so what?

Shane Sr, meanwhile, was having to take any job that was offered to cover the mortgage and that meant his son and I spent the majority of my time on our own. The saving grace of that period was that Shane Jr's noisy entrance of crying was literally a false alarm and, once he'd got it out of his system, he spent the next twelve months or so doing little else but eating, pooing his nappy and sleeping.

Funnily enough, and this relates back to the morning sickness mystery, Maureen became pregnant just after I did and we had our boys about five weeks apart. I was able to go up and visit her with Shane when her son, Danny, arrived and it was nice to be able to share some of those early days with somebody close. I know I told this story in my first book but I remember coming down in the morning with Shane at Maureen's house while she was coming up the stairs with Danny.

'Is this the first time you've been up since last night?' she said, looking exhausted.

'I'm afraid so,' I replied, trying not to look smug!

'I hate you and I want to swap children!' said Maureen.

Of course, Danny wasn't doing anything out of the ordinary for a child his age, it was Shane who was. Not that I was complaining! Maureen got her revenge, though. From the age of one Shane suddenly took a vow of wakefulness and refused to sleep. Talk about being lulled into a false sense of security! It literally happened overnight. One night he was superchild who always slept through and was no bother, and the next he was like something out of the sodding *Omen* on half a dozen Pro Plus!

The person to blame for this dreadful change is actually Michael Jackson. Shane became obsessed with his film, *Moonwalker*, and I have awful memories of sitting up at four o'clock in the morning with him, watching it for the umpteenth time. I used to think to myself, Save me somebody! The only positive was that it stopped me worrying about Shane Jr sleeping so much, which I had been doing previously! Why on earth would you worry about a baby sleeping? Well, I managed it.

To be fair, I did actually have grounds for worrying as, when he was three weeks old, I put him to bed one night at 10 p.m. and at 1 p.m. the following day he was still spark out! I kept going up to his room every five minutes to check that he was breathing. I remember calling my mum. 'Ooh, you don't know you're born, Coleen,' she said. 'If he wants to sleep, let him!'

Let's lighten the mood and talk about baby names! For all three of mine, I went for quite normal names (well, I thought so, anyway!). Shane was named after his dad, a tradition in my family, and Jake and Ciara we just liked. These days you hear all sorts of names and sometimes it makes my blood boil. I mean, what about the poor child? You're not the one who'll have to go to school and tell everyone that you're named after a bloody number or something. I also don't understand naming your child after the place where they were conceived, which in Shane Jr's case would be Downstairs Toilet: Downstairs Toilet Roach, or W. C. Roach. I don't know.

My own name caused me a whole heap of problems when I went to school. Not because it was particularly weird, but because it just wasn't very common in England. Had I gone to school in Ireland it would have been fine but in Blackpool people used to say, 'What are you called? *Colin*? That's a funny name for a girl.' I got bullied through the whole of primary school because of 'Coleen' and, by the time I left, I hated my name. I used to give myself pseudonyms when I went out as a teenager. 'Hi, my name's Julie.' Anything but bloody 'Colin'!

My own experience of motherhood changed me in the way I felt. I wasn't just Coleen any more, I was someone's mum. All of a sudden, I felt grown up and that was obviously caused by the sense of responsibility that comes with having a baby. It wasn't that I'd been what you'd call irresponsible before that, I'd just never had anyone who relied on me before. Apart from Shane Sr, of course. When Shane Jr came along that meant I had two flatulent and annoying little bastards to look after!

When Shane Jr got to being two years old, he started having daily tantrums that would last about two hours. Screaming, kicking, scratching. You know the kind of thing. Because he was my first-born I used to spend those two hours going, 'Do you want this? How about this? For fuck's sake, tell me what you want!' I'd try everything. By the time Jake came along, I'd realised that all they actually want is to have a bloody tantrum and let off some steam. So, when Jake started going off on one I'd just carry on with what I was doing and he'd be done in twenty minutes. Doddle! Toddlers like an audience and as soon as they realise that they're not going to get one, they shut up.

As I said earlier, as soon as my children started to move, they became annoying in my eyes. Well, not completely – but a bit. I loved being pregnant and loved the very early days, but as soon as they started to become mobile, that was it. Before that, if anyone said, 'Do you want me to have them for an hour?' I wasn't all that bothered. When they became toddlers, though, I'd have handed them over with some nappies and a bottle before whoever had been daft enough to offer had finished the question. I was out! All the same, I do get the cuteness of when they're toddlers. You know, saying the wrong words and stuff. It's just the constant movement that bugs me. There's no respite!

When Shane first sat up on his own it was a momentous occasion and, instantly, I thought, Ooh, I can't wait until he can crawl! Then, as soon as he crawled, I couldn't wait until he could walk. When Jake came along, I remember him pulling himself up on the arm of the couch one day and I very gently took his legs from under him. I'd realised what I'd done with Shane Jr, you see, and I wanted to savour every moment of immobility: you'll start walking when I tell you, young man!

When Jake was born Shane Jr was all over him like a rash and, for the first two years or so, he wouldn't leave him alone. He wanted to feed him and put him to bed. It was so sweet. Then, when Jake was two and Shane was six, Jake started interfering with whatever his big brother was doing and that's when the problems started.

That was yet another learning curve as a parent because, until then, it had actually been OK. Well, on and off. Having two kids is obviously harder than having one but, if they're at each other's throats all the time, it takes it to a very different level.

Jake was also ten days late, by the way, and so was Ciara. Isn't that strange? I remember being quite confident when Jake arrived, though. How much harder could it be having two kids instead of one? I asked myself. By far the worst part was when they both needed attention at the same time. That actually brought me to tears quite a few times and used to leave me in a state of despair. I remember I was feeding Jake on the couch once, when Shane started crying for something. I thought, I don't know what to do! Bernie came over soon after that for a few days and, at one point, I just sat on the couch and started sobbing in front of her. I felt a mixture of desperation, helplessness, frustration and despair. It was horrid!

By the time Ciara came along, Jake was eight and Shane was twelve and that was a whole different ballgame! In fact, you could say that the stars had all aligned. For a start, Ciara was a girl and the boys absolutely adored having a sister. There was also no sibling rivalry because of the age gap. Best of all, though, I was now thirty-six years old and, as well as having a bit of experience under my belt, I also had the right temperament. In fact, I'd go as far as to say that I was calmness personified! Nothing fazed me. Ray, on the other hand, was absolutely all over the place, as this was his first child. Fortunately, because I'd been there, I knew how to calm him down. Rub brandy on his gums!

Reading this next bit is going to make some of you a little sick; throughout her childhood and teenage years, Ciara didn't throw a single tantrum. Not one! It sounds unbelievable, really, but it's true. What makes it stranger still is that she's now almost twenty and she *still* hasn't had one. Nor have I ever had to shout at her or tell her off. She's so calm and so measured. I don't know where she gets it from! Certainly not me. Then again, I don't really argue with people and Ray tends to bottle everything up, so perhaps she is a chip off the old block? She'd sit for hours, sometimes, while I had friends around and you wouldn't hear a peep out of her. Everyone would go, 'Where the hell did you get her from?'

Ciara was the only one of the three I breastfed and, as I've already said, I hated every second of it! I only did it because Ray wanted me to. He kept going on and on about how important it was and I thought, OK, I'll give it a go. What I didn't realise was that, unlike bottle-feeding, it's feed-on-demand with boobs and, because Ciara was such a big baby – 9 lb 4 oz – she was constantly hungry. What I should have done was express as much milk as possible and say to Ray, 'Here you go. You get up every two bloody hours!'

It was the same with dummies. Ray didn't want her to use one and I said, 'OK, *you* sit and listen to her crying constantly for half an hour, because I'm not.' That's why they're called pacifiers, for heaven's sake! I'm not saying I used one all the time but for the sake of my own sanity I sometimes popped one in and, in hindsight, I wish I'd given one to Ray and Shane too!

Just remember, it's not just, 'What's best for baby,' it's, 'What's best for you and baby.'

One of the reasons Ciara was so ridiculously laidback was that I was an experienced mum by then. I'd done the whole panicking parent bit by the time she arrived and had moved into second-nature mode. Had I been running around and pulling my hair out, things might have been different. In fact, I'm sure they would! Thank God for that age difference, though, as if she'd been just a year or two behind the boys or even four or five, I'd have been in trouble and I might not be talking about the three of them quite so warmly!

I'll tell you something else I did that made a difference. With the boys, I always tried putting them to bed at a certain time that I thought was right. It was usually about seven o'clock but, by the time they actually went to sleep, it was at least nine. Every night I did the same thing and every night I spent at least two hours battling with them and trying to send them off to the land of nod. With Ciara I did the opposite. Instead of me telling her when it was time for bed she used to tell me. I'm not saying that would work with every child – if I'd tried it with Shane and Jake they'd have stayed up until around midnight. With Ciara it was different and, as opposed to fighting the tiredness or ignoring it, she'd just come up to me and go, 'I'm tired now,' and I'd take her up to bed. There was no fight and no arguing. It was bliss!

I'd probably have had at least one more baby if Ray had been up for it. One was enough for him and so, after Ciara, I pulled the shutters down and shut up shop! I'd have another one tomorrow though, if it was safe for me to do so and if I was able to – if I was about twenty years younger! I'd need a man for that, though, and although I wouldn't say no to another baby, having another man around would be a different proposition. I couldn't cope with both! Being pregnant has given me some of the happiest times of my life. It all felt very natural at the time.

Pre-ordained, almost. You don't hear many women say that now, do you? God, I'm strange!

Before we move on, let me just give you a favourite memory of each of them as children. With Shane and Jake it's me walking into the living room after I'd bathed them to find Jake sitting on Shane Jr's knee, drinking his bottle and watching television, while Shane Jr played with his hair. That melted my heart and, although it wouldn't be long before they started kicking the shit out of each other, it was nice while it lasted.

One of my favourite memories of Ciara came courtesy of a video that Ray sent me one day while I was working on *This Morning*. She was toddling and still wearing a nappy and the video showed her trying to climb into the washing machine. The only thing stopping her was the fact that the nappy was too big and, when I first saw the clip, I melted! It was such a heartwarming moment. I'm always watching videos of kids doing either cute or daft things on Instagram. It's my not-very-guilty pleasure!

That's the thing about kids though. One minute they can drive you absolutely insane and the next they can have you rolling on the floor wetting yourself laughing or melting like Mr or Mrs Soppy-Pants. Making memories is probably one of the most important things you can do as a parent, though, as once they've flown the nest it's sometimes all you have left from that period of time. Well, that and stretch-bloody-marks!

I think I should impart a few words of motherly wisdom to anybody who's had kids and is struggling with them.

The first thing I'd say is, stop stressing about trying to be the perfect mum or dad. There's no such thing as a perfect parent and all you can ever do is your best. However inadequate that might seem sometimes, trust me, it isn't!

Something else I'd say is that it's more important for a child to fit into your routine than you to fit into theirs. I know it's often tempting to let them lead, but the more comfortable you are, the more energy and enthusiasm you'll have when times get tough. That attitude turned out to be a godsend for me, especially with Shane Jr. It's not an exact science, though. God, no! Each one of my three children were completely different. They had different wants, different needs, different habits and different personalities.

If I'd read a book on parenting and had stuck to the letter it might well have caused me and my kids irreparable damage. Being a parent is a constant learning process and the best gift you can give to your child – and to yourself, as well – is a willingness to adapt. Just remember, whatever feels right for you and your child.

Lastly, if you hear a mum or a dad waffling on and on about how wonderful and perfect their beautiful little children are, and how they would never ever give them anything as disgusting or harmful as junk food, blah, blah, blah ... for God's sake don't be tempted to get into a conversation with them. Just tell them to piss off!

Being a single parent

I obviously spent a good few years as a single parent and, although I've mentioned it elsewhere in the book, I thought I'd give it a small section of its own, especially as it's always something I've been asked about a lot, both at the *Mirror* and when I meet people.

It's also something we've talked about a lot on *Loose Women* over the years. Mind you, is there anything we *haven't* talked about on *Loose Women?* We actually had a discussion about tomato plants the other day – yes, tomato plants – and while Janet and Brenda were getting all excited I walked off set to make Ruth and me a cuppa because I was so bored!

Becoming a single parent is even more daunting than becoming a mum for the first time. Once again, you're taking a trip into the unknown but this time you're alone. Not surprisingly, some of the strongest people I've ever met have been mums whose partners buggered off before their child was born or who didn't actually have a close relationship with the dad. Or they just had a one-night stand! Let's not pretend these things never happen. Anyway, women who are on their own from the off obviously have to learn quickly and the ones who learn to thrive in that environment are just super-women.

I've got a very good friend who's in exactly that situation and I look at her as a kind of warrior. Nothing phases her. In fact, if she said to me that she was thinking of invading a country and taking it over single-handed, I'd believe her!

She just gets her head down and gets on with things. She said a while ago that she and her son wouldn't even think about having a man on the scene as he'd just get on their nerves. All they've ever known is each other and they're so incredibly close. They've also got a routine going and they don't want anyone messing that up.

I'm certainly not putting myself in my friend's bracket but, before Shane and I split up, I was left on my own an awful lot and by the time the relationship came to an end I at least had an inkling of what was involved. What I wasn't prepared for, however, was how it would make me feel. Not fully. To put it bluntly, I absolutely crapped myself! Not for very long, but when we went our separate ways and I was left with the boys I did get that familiar feeling that I'd felt as a new mum once or twice: what the bloody hell do I do now? Had I not had a good relationship with Shane, that feeling would have been a hell of a lot worse I should imagine. As it was, he was very supportive generally and it was OK.

This will surprise you but, having had a cuppa and thought about it (for about the thousandth time!), I'd say that being on your own is better, in some ways, as sometimes having a husband or partner is like having another child to look after. If that grown-up 'child' does bugger off, it means you can concentrate on the smaller ones! They'll probably kill me for saying it, but I'd put both my ex-husbands into that category. Seriously, they were so, so difficult to look after. More so than the kids, in many ways. And they certainly smelled just as bad!

When it was just me and the kids, I could actually just get on with things a lot of the time, instead of having to look after Shane or Ray and worry about what they'd think and say about stuff. It's swings and roundabouts, I suppose. Obviously, there are benefits to having a husband or a partner around when you're bringing up children, but there are minuses too. Big ones!

I'm speaking as somebody who has never been in what you might call a conventional marriage so, before you start packing your other half's suitcase and telling him that Coleen says, 'You have to bugger off,' just you hold your horses! With Shane, I genuinely did feel like I was already a single parent most of the time and not just because he was away an awful lot. Even when he was at home he was no help, as he'd never do nappies – any of the messy stuff – or housework. I'm talking about practical issues – when it came to emotional support, he was slightly better, when he was around. But as important as emotional backup is, it's not going to feed a child three times a night, clean the house and do the washing, is it? Practical assistance is essential. Ray, bless him, was so hands on with Ciara that I barely had to lift a finger!

That's the reason I moved back to Blackpool after Shane and I split – my family were there. I obviously needed to work and I wasn't going to leave the boys with just anyone. I could also call on lots of emotional support, if I needed it. Just being close to my family was fabulous. It gave me a lovely sense of security and, although I hadn't realised it, that was something else I'd been missing.

Live. Laugh. Love.

I think the trick to making it work when you're bringing up children on your own while still being in contact with the father, is being able to strike a balance between what's best for everyone involved, not just for the children, but for both parents. This is especially true for the person chiefly looking after the kids! The other parent, who doesn't need to deal with all the crap full-time, should be prepared to make allowances. Not everyone does, though. In fact, if I had a pound for every letter I've had at the *Mirror* from people whose other halves are refusing to get involved and/or is expecting to live the life of somebody who is basically young, free and single, I'd be able to buy a herd of bloody pygmy goats! It makes my blood boil when I read these letters. I'd give them such a rocket!

What you have to watch out for if you're the one left holding the baby or babies, so to speak, is getting into a good-cop/bad-cop situation. Let me explain. If your ex comes around at the weekend and takes the kids out, he or she will often, basically, let them do whatever the hell they want. It's understandable, I suppose, and is driven by a mixture of guilt and wanting to ensure that they have a good time. I get it!

What you have to watch out for – and I bet loads of you have experienced this – is the kids then putting your cheating ratbag of an ex on a pedestal because they've allowed them to eat sweets all day and say rude words. The kids then resent you because you've got to deal with the aftermath by getting them to bed and dealing with all the crap.

As well as being incredibly unfair, it's also tremendously frustrating.

When Shane used to pick up the boys at the weekend I'd say to him, 'Right, then. Jake's not allowed to have loads of sweets because he's been naughty and Shane Jr can't go to the zoo because he blew up the science lab again.' You know the kind of thing. Yet, on each occasion, Shane would, basically, take the boys out and do whatever I'd asked him not to. Not to be spiteful or anything. He just couldn't resist saying, 'Yes,' to his sons. When they got back at the end of the day the boys would leap out of the car and say, 'Mum, we've been to the zoo and had loads of sweets!' After which I would give Shane one of my looks!

If you're experiencing something similar, you really should try and sit down and talk it through. Shane and I did and, although it took a while, we finally came to an understanding. He wanted to give the kids a good time, which I accepted, and I didn't want to be undermined, which he also accepted. In fact, not only did I not want to be undermined but I wanted to be supported. We agreed that, if I said that the boys couldn't do something, Shane would find something else to do (or eat!) that was equally exciting. At the end of the day, Shane Sr had the ability to sell ice to the flaming Eskimos; persuading two excited kids that ice-cream is better than sweets or that the seaside is better than the zoo shouldn't be too difficult.

The hardest part of being a single parent was building my career again and providing for the kids, at least, the first time around. I was lucky in the sense that I didn't have to worry too much about money at first, as Shane was doing well, but I had no idea how long that would last. What if it all went tits up? Then where would we be?

When we moved back to Blackpool, instead of using the divorce money to buy a biggish house that would probably also require a mortgage, I decided to buy a smaller home outright. That way, if Shane ever had any problems with money, it would affect us three less. I know that sounds a bit ruthless but that's how you think in those kind of situations. It's how you have to think. You're basically in survival mode. Equally, I knew that if I had trouble restarting my career, at least we'd have a roof over our heads, no matter what.

In the end, that move turned out to be a masterstroke – she says modestly – as it took me ages to find any work. Or, at least, any steady work. I was scraping around, basically, doing bits and pieces here and there. I obviously didn't know this at that time, but I'd end up in the same boat after *This Morning* except, when it first happened, after Shane, I was on my own and had far less experience, both professionally and personally. In fact, in the eyes of any future employers at the time I was basically just a Nolan Sister who hadn't worked for a few years. What did I have to offer?

Realising the reality of my situation, I started looking for jobs outside of showbusiness; any ambitions I might have had within the industry went completely out of the window. I just needed to work! As you know, within a few months I'd been offered *Celebrity Heartbreak* and the rest is history. It still took a long time to establish myself, though; the worries about providing for the kids and remaining solvent didn't go away.

The first piece of advice I'd offer any single parent is that you should never be too proud to ask for help and if anyone offers you assistance, take it. Asking for or accepting help is often judged a sign of failure, but only by the people who need it. Those offering help don't see it that way, at least, not in my experience. Just remember the old saying that pride comes before a fall and what matters far more than pride is what's best for you and your kids. In fact, in that situation, nothing matters more. Just remember that there are people out there who, if you didn't ask them for help, would be absolutely gutted. So just do it!

The other piece of advice I'd give, which has become a bit of a running theme throughout this book, is to talk to people about your worries and fears. Becoming a single parent can be one of the most daunting things you can have to face in life and telling people how you feel – especially people who might have been there too – will definitely help. The worst thing you can do in this situation is to bottle things up.

Also, don't forget to talk to your kids about what's happening. They can obviously be affected deeply by their parents splitting up and they're often forgotten about. It may not be intentional, but just remember that you're all in this together and, by making sure that everyone feels comfortable talking about it, you'll be doing yourselves a big favour.

Moving on – introducing a step-parent

Introducing a step-parent, or a potential step-parent, can be almost as daunting as becoming a single parent and how it goes will have a lot to do with the relationship you have with your kids. You see what I mean by talking to kids? If your lines of communication are rubbish then you could be in for all kinds of trouble. When a new person arrives on the scene, the kids might feel isolated and that's the last thing you want. The more they feel they can approach you with their problems, the better. It's not easy, though.

When I first started seeing Ray, all those years ago, I told the boys that he was just a friend of mine, at least, at first. Shane Jr wasn't having any of it, though. He must have been eleven at the time and Jake seven, and I remember him saying, 'Yeah, of *course* he's your friend, Mum. Sure!' The reason I told them both that Ray and I were just friends was because I was terrified of Jake's reaction but, fortunately – unlike Shane – he was none the wiser.

I was afraid because Jake had become very possessive of me since I split up with Shane and we had to tread carefully. Unfortunately, this approach was scuppered when I found out that I was pregnant just two months after Ray and I started seeing each other. I went from having to tell Jake that I'd met somebody new to having to explain that I'd met somebody new *and* he was also going to be a big brother!

I remember the day I first broached it with Jake like it was yesterday. All four of us were having fish and chips and I said, 'Jake, how would you feel if I ever had another baby?'

'Well,' he said. 'I think I'd just pack my bags, run away and you'd never see me again.' As soon as he'd finished talking, both Ray and Shane Jr stood up and walked out and I remember thinking, Oh, my God! What am I going to do?

The next morning, while I was getting Jake ready for school, I said, 'Did you mean what you said, about running away if I had another baby?' and he said, 'Why? Are you pregnant?'

'Yes,' I said. 'I am.' I just had to come out with it.

Do you know what? He flung his arms around me, ran out of the front door and to two complete strangers he said, 'My mum's having a baby!'

When I arrived at the front door, this man and women looked at me and went, 'Congratulations!'

The slightly scary thing here is that, if I'd been just thinking about having a baby rather than being pregnant and Jake had said he'd run away, I probably wouldn't have had another child. Yet, less than twenty-four hours later, he was in love with the idea and incredibly happy. I'm pleased to report that this carried on throughout the pregnancy and, when Ciara was born, Jake was obsessed with her. It was such a relief, though, as I was expecting fireworks. Big ones! I remember calling the entire family and telling them about Jake's reaction and they were all in floods of tears. Or, at least, the sisters were.

The first couple of years of my relationship with Ray were very difficult for me with the kids and, if it hadn't been for Ciara coming along, we wouldn't have lasted. That might sound quite dramatic, but it's the truth. Everybody has to find the line in a family when a new boyfriend or girlfriend arrives on the scene and sometimes the aftermath gets to be too much. Emotionally, I was pulled from pillar to post, time and time again and, although I wanted to be supportive of Ray, I found it very hard sometimes. It's no fun being in the middle, that's for sure!

One thing I was very careful not to do was let the kids hear Ray and I arguing, especially if it was about them, which it was, sometimes. Once they hear arguments then they have control of the situation and, although they're only kids, they'll use it to their advantage.

Once again, if I had to give any advice to somebody who was having trouble introducing a new boyfriend or girlfriend, I'd say keep those lines of communication open. Twenty-four hours a day if necessary! Today, if I ever had to tell Ciara about a new boyfriend – a serious one – she'd probably want to vet him first. In fact, I'd probably ask her to! She actually knows more about my love life than anyone else and, if she didn't think that a new boyfriend was right for me, I'm not sure it would work. She'd never actually tell me not to see somebody (unless she'd seen him on the news or in the papers, of course!), but she's a really good judge of character. And, let's face it, with my track record, somebody's got to take bloody charge!

I'd also advise people to establish the line of what is acceptable and what isn't as soon as possible with a new partner, especially for the kids. One thing you can't do is introduce a new adult into a family and then say, 'By the way, I don't want you disciplining my children.' If you do that, the moment you leave the room the kids will start giving your new other half shit, knowing full well that they can get away with it. That's why talking is so, so important in these situations. It might be uncomfortable, sometimes, but so what?

Your kids won't like being disciplined by somebody new and they'll probably come out with lines such as, 'He's not my real dad!' or, 'She's not my real mum!' You know the kind of thing. Unless you're lucky and have kids who are basically angels then it'll probably be quite a long process and you have to stick at it. You have to stay strong! I know exactly how tempting it is to cave in and side with your kids but, even if you're doing that just for a quiet life, you could end up with anything but.

Had I been with Ray and had Ciara not come along then he'd probably have left. In fact, I know he would. Jake's obsession with me made things very, very hard for Ray and, as I said, that phase lasted about two years. We had tantrums, screaming fits and all the usual 'You're not my dad' stuff. It was relentless. We also had accusations that I loved Ray more than I loved him. Predictable, given the circumstances but, when you actually hear your child say something like that (or, should I say, scream it!), you really feel the effect.

Things got so bad that we ended up having family counselling. There'll be some people who scoff at the idea but, if ever there was a need for an impartial ear and some good old-fashioned common sense, this was it. Jake was so incredibly angry, which was what made us seek help. Ray made the point that if we didn't get it sorted now, what would happen when Jake was fifteen and six foot tall? All of us needed to speak to somebody impartial, but no one needed it more than Jake. At last, he could try putting into words why he was feeling so furious all the time, and the counsellor was able to teach him coping mechanisms.

I think the main problem people have with family counselling – and it's same with one-to-one counselling – is opening up to a stranger. I suppose it is counter-intuitive in a way, opening up emotionally to someone you don't know, but the fact of the matter is that if they weren't a stranger it simply wouldn't work.

The idea of a family having counselling thirty or forty years ago would probably have been ridiculed but in our case, not only did it help Jake overcome his anger, it also helped us understand why he was angry and why he was acting in the way he was, which enabled us to help him. I shudder to think what would have happened had we not had counselling. It wouldn't have ended well, though.

Let me just put all this into context by telling you what happened afterwards, shall I? Basically, both Shane Jr and Jake grew to adore Ray and, despite the fact that we're no longer married, that hasn't changed one bit. Jake's now twenty-nine and he always says that had Ray not stuck around then he doesn't know what would have happened.

He certainly wouldn't be as good-natured and well-behaved as he is. Sometimes! I was quite soft, you see, and despite all the crap at the beginning, Ray really was the one who ended up disciplining Jake. If he grounded Jake for a week, which he used to do all the time, it would last for a week, no exceptions. If it had been left up to me, I'd have relented the following day or when Jake started behaving himself again.

Sometimes I'd say, 'Oh, come on, Ray. He's said he's sorry. Let him go out.'

'If I do that once,' Ray would say, 'then he won't think I mean what I say and that will affect the way he behaves.' He was absolutely right, of course, and Jake's behaviour improved because Ray stuck to his guns.

Just remember, if you're in a situation where you're introducing a potential step-parent into your family, as well as talking, do yourself a favour and don't rule anything out as a means for finding help, especially counselling.

Flying the nest
(finally getting rid of the little sods!)

As you'll know by now, my kids haven't actually flown the nest yet (well, I suppose Shane Jr and Jake did, briefly, but they seem to have returned!) and you might be wondering what makes me qualified to give advice. Well, I gave my opinions on religion but I'm not a priest!

The funny thing is, I experienced empty nest syndrome when my kids hit eighteen, despite them still living at home!

Live. Laugh. Love.

How daft is that? Looking back, this feeling had been chipping away at me for years. You know – when they learn to use the washing machine for the first time or go and get the shopping. Each step brings them closer to not needing me any more and, ultimately – although it hasn't happened yet – flying the nest. By the time they reached eighteen and became adults I was a gibbering wreck; God knows what I'll be like when they eventually leave!

I never used to understand empty nest syndrome and, when the kids were little, I always claimed that when they finally departed for good I'd be partying every night. That's genuinely what I thought, though. The house will be clean and I can watch what I want on TV. I can even go to bed when I want! It was a win-win situation as far as I was concerned.

I forget when it actually began but, one day, Shane Jr did something for himself (for a change!) which tipped the balance. I'd assumed they would always need me and now I could see them becoming independent. It's been like a countdown ever since and, as much as I try and fight against it, it's obviously inevitable.

As well as missing them, which I obviously will when they leave home, I'm afraid of feeling redundant. It's similar to the way the menopause made me feel as a woman, except this time this relates to me as a mother and, in many ways, that's worse. Shane Jr's getting married next year, so he'll definitely be going. That'll be my first test. I wonder how I'll cope? I expect I'll mention it on *Loose Women*. If I do, expect tears!

One of the biggest about-turns, with regard to the way my mind processed the kids getting older, came when Ciara finished high school. In the weeks before, all I could think about was the prospect of not having to do the school run ever again. Then, when I finally dropped her off for the last time, I bawled my eyes out! Not just because she was getting older, but because it was such a landmark moment for both of us. Ciara had finished school, which was huge for her, and I'd been doing the school run five days a week for over twenty years! It was the proverbial end of an era, really, although I must admit that by the following Monday morning, when I didn't have to get out of bed, the tears had dried up! It was a strange feeling, though, knowing that I'd never have to do another school run ever again.

The next event that pulled on my heartstrings in that way was Ciara passing her driving test. I went from never needing to do the school run again to never even having to give her a sodding lift! I'd spent half my life driving kids everywhere, up to when they reached early adulthood. As I'm not a drinker I'd always be the one who'd give them a lift back from the pub or from a party. Now what was I going to do? Coleen's Cabs was about to go out of business!

Parenthood provides you with so many moments like that and the effect they have will obviously vary, depending on how you interpret life events. It's difficult not to get a bit nostalgic and even a bit tearful when you drop your youngest off at school for the last time but, equally, there's bugger all you can do about it. Also, look at it from your kid's point of view: they're going to be so excited by what's happening; despite the nostalgia pulling at your heart-strings, it's all good. I think what I'm actually trying to say is that, ultimately, it's not about you, it's about them. Equally, as much as it might hurt you to see them leaving the nest, it won't stop them needing you. You'll just get a phone call asking you for money instead of being pestered in person!

I love mothering my kids (I'll mother anybody's kids!) and, to this day, it's ultimately what gets me up in the morning. Yes, I know they're all fairly self-sufficient but, even if they don't need me for anything in particular, just being there for them in case they do gives me a purpose in life. Saying you feel redundant when your kids get older or fly the nest isn't just a figure of speech, especially if you're a mum. To all intents and purposes, you are losing your job for real – a job that you might have dedicated yourself to for twenty years or more. Being made redundant is never nice. This is why it's important that, if you are about to experience empty nest syndrome, you should try and have a goal in mind, not necessarily something to replace your kids, but to distract you from the fact that they're no longer around. Why do you think I've got so many animals?!

I'll tell you what's also important, and that's forming and maintaining good relationships with your kids' part-ners, if you can. In some cases, it can be impossible, but even if you don't particularly like the person you should at least try and find some common ground. I've been very fortunate in that department, but I know lots of people who haven't and, as the child usually ends up siding with their partner, the parents will end up suffering. You might have to bite your tongue sometimes, but falling out with your child because you don't like their choice of partner is rarely worth it. Of course, if you have concerns for your child's welfare, no matter how old they are, then you should step in. If they're not listening to you, try and get someone like their dad or a trusted aunt/uncle/family friend, who might be able to get through.

I think the most important thing I've done in countering empty nest syndrome is reminding myself that, whatever happens, I'll always be their mum. When I left home, I still needed my mum. Even now, if I'm ever feeling ill, I'll say to the kids, 'I want my mum!' 'Erm, you might have a bit of a problem there,' they always reply.

And if that doesn't work, buy yourself some pygmy goats or a dog!

How to be a goddess in
every area of your life

The thought of me being any kind of goddess – domestic, sex or otherwise – makes me wet myself laughing but other celebs pretend they are, so, why shouldn't I? I suppose I could be a tea goddess – but sex and cleaning? I'll say one thing about sex, though, I always try my hardest! I do have some experiences to share with you, obviously, not to mention some opinions, so here goes. Prepare to be transformed!

Domestic goddess

When I clean the house from top to bottom I get an immediate sense of achievement but, if the house is still clean, after a few hours I start to hate it. You see, if my house is clean it means there's nobody home but me and I'm not used to being left home alone. Fortunately, that doesn't happen very often and, when I do clean the house, it tends to recapture its 'lived-in' quality quite quickly. For me, that's what makes a home special: not massive TVs, expensive furniture, manicured gardens or clean worktops.

Live. Laugh. Love.

I've said previously that I'm not really a material sort of person – it's the feeling I get just walking through my front door that makes me incredibly happy. In fact, I've got a plaque on the wall in my kitchen that says, 'Home is not a place, it's a feeling'. It doesn't matter what's been going on that day; when I arrive home, the moment I close the door behind me, any stress melts away. What actually creates feelings of happiness and contentment I couldn't tell you, but it's probably a mixture of things. As corny as the saying is, there really is no place like home.

When I was growing up, ten of us lived together in a three-bedroom, terraced house, along with a never-ending stream of visitors. I know it's a bit of a cliché but, in those days, you literally did have people walking in your kitchen door, unannounced, for a chat and a cup of tea. Our house was absolute chaos almost all of the time and, having thought about it, that's probably the magic element when it comes to making a home. It's not the place itself or even the possessions that matter so much, it's the people inside it.

For some people, it's the other way around. I know lots of people who are what you'd call 'house proud' and, if you added an element of chaos into the mix, they'd go mad. Don't get me wrong, I couldn't cope with a chaotic house twenty-four-seven, but I could manage twenty-one-seven, no problem! When I was young, my ambition was always to spend more time at home, to see my family and play with my friends and nothing's changed really – except that my family are now my children and my friends are all animals.

I'm sometimes asked if I have any guilty pleasures at home. The only one I can think of really is being a slob. Actually, that should have been the title of this section, 'Slob Goddess'! I really am *that* good, especially now I'm single. I no longer have to worry about somebody seeing me and thinking, Look at the state of you! As soon as I get home, I chuck my bag on the floor, run upstairs, take my makeup off, put my hair in a ponytail, put my pyjamas on, run downstairs, make a cup of tea and start enjoying life. Seriously, I could not give a toss!

Getting back to the domestic goddess theme for a second, what about things like Christmas? That's when a real domestic goddess should come into her own. Once again, it all depends on your definition of what makes a domestic goddess, really. My own image, although she would have hated the idea of being called a domestic goddess, is my mum. Christmas, in particular, was the time when she really came into her own in that department and, to this day, I'm still in complete awe of the way that she did it.

Christmas at our house was fantastic; it was – and still is – my favourite time of year. Fortunately, my enthusiasm seems to have rubbed off on the kids. They love it just as much. I'm getting my cliché bag out again, but Christmas is such a magical time!

We used to have between twenty-four and twenty-six people for Christmas dinner in our tiny little home, which was where the domestic goddess thing comes in. We'd have aunties, cousins, friends – the lot. It was chaos of the very best kind and my mum used to cook single-handedly, on a tiny gas cooker. There was no dishwasher and no freezer; everything was fresh. Dealing with all that is what makes a domestic goddess! Most amazingly of all, she never ever became stressed and I only appreciated how amazing it all was – and how amazing she was – when I started doing it myself.

The first time I cooked Christmas dinner I left the giblets in the turkey and could have killed us all, but you live and learn. Or you live and die, if I'm in charge! I'm a crap cook. I *can* cook but I just don't care enough. Apart from the usual meat-and-two-veg stuff I don't stray too far. Ask me to do a sauce and I'll just tell you where the ketchup is. The thing is, because I was the youngest of our family, I never had to worry about cooking and in that respect I was a bit spoiled.

Should I tell you what Christmas at Coleen's is like? Well, last Christmas, Shane's fiancée, Maddy, cooked. It was her suggestion that she do it and, from the way she asked, I think she thought I was going to be against the idea. 'Go for your bloody life!' I said to her. It turned out to be one of the best Christmas dinners I've ever had – so she's made a rod for her own back.

The only real traditions I have, apart from spending an entire day putting up my six Christmas trees with Ciara, which I love, is that the Christmas 24 channel will be constantly on from October and I'll play at least one Christmas album every day. Apart from that, it's just a mass of tea, alcohol and calories!

My favourite Christmas song of all time is 'Have Yourself a Merry Little Christmas' – the version sung by Frank Sinatra. When I was young, me and my sisters learnt it in five-part harmony and every Christmas, to this day, we all sing it. It conjures up so many wonderful memories from those Christmases in Blackpool. The kids always go, 'Oh, God, not again!' For us girls, though, it's incredibly special. I love all Christmas songs, really, and Christmas films. My favourite seasonal movies when I was growing up were the original version of *The Miracle on 34th Street* and *It's a Wonderful Life*, but I also love the newer ones like *The Santa Clause* and *Elf*. I like the movies in which Santa turns out to be real. I always sit there and think, Yes! I knew he was! I'm such a child when it comes to Christmas. On Christmas Eve, I still look out of the window before I got to bed to see if he's coming, even though I've just put all the presents out myself! It's daft, isn't it?

What else are domestic goddesses supposed to be good at. Sewing? Not me. *Loose Women* challenged me to sew on a button during one of the breaks when it came out that I'd never done it before. They were shocked that I'd got this far in life without even sewing a single button.

'But I'm the youngest of eight,' I said. 'I didn't have to, so I never learned.'

'Well, you've had kids,' they said. 'What happened when a button came off their trousers?'

'I'd go to Tesco and buy some new ones,' I replied, 'or, if it was a shirt, I'd get them to roll their sleeves up!'

I did actually manage to sew the button on during the break, by the way, so there is a domestic goddess in there somewhere. She's just very well hidden!

Having read all that, I suppose you're now waiting for me to give you my tips on how to be a domestic goddess? First, get yourself a cleaner, a cook and a gardener . . . Then put your pyjamas on, lock the front door, turn your phone off and get the bloody gin out! Or, if you're not charging your kids rent, get them to do everything! Seriously, though, I could never have a cleaner; I'd be too embarrassed and would have to clean before they arrived. Nobody should have to witness my squalor, let alone clean it up for me!

My main tip then for how to be a domestic goddess is don't. If anyone's coming round who might judge you, tell them you've had a better offer! Seriously, just slob out, enjoy yourself, and balls to the lot of them!

Sex goddess (this'll be good!)

This is going to be the closest I've come to writing fiction in this book as persuading anybody that I'm a sex goddess is going to require – how can I put it? – one or two massive bloody lies! Yet again, it all depends on your definition of a sex goddess. I suppose my job here is to persuade you that it's me. Christ on a bike!

My interest in boys started when I was quite young. There was a boy at primary school called Phillip who all the girls fancied. He was in the year above me and seemed very mature. Whenever we played kiss chase, I would always refuse to run! He was my first crush, I suppose. I had my first actual boyfriend when I was fifteen and I stayed with him for four years. You know what I mean by 'actual' boyfriend, don't you? As in, we had lots of special cuddles and things.

The way I've always managed to attract men – apart from using my amazing sense of humour, my stunning good looks and my ginormous boobs – is by flirting. I've always been a great flirter but I'm actually quite cowardly, in that I'll flirt and flirt and flirt, and then think, Oh, Christ, he's taken me seriously! After that, I'll panic, unless I'm with somebody I really fancy. If that's the case, they won't know what's hit them!

I'll take any opportunity, though. When the postman comes I'll have a little flirt and the kids will go, 'Mother, it's the postman. Put him down!' My flirting is always innuendo-based and when the postman brings a parcel I might say, 'My word, that's a big one. Are you going to put it in my box for me?' You know the sort of thing. It's like a scene from a *Carry On* film. If the postman flirts back, though, I literally turn into a five-year-old! I'm like, 'Oh God, no, I'm only messing!' When I genuinely fancy somebody I'm not capable of flirting – or speaking, for that matter. My kids find this hilarious and immediately start taking the piss. 'Poor man,' they say. 'Shall we warn him?'

The qualities that I find the most attractive in men now are a sense of humour and talent, but in the early days it was usually more about the talent. Musicians were my weakness; my first love was a performer. He used to play the piano for me and I'd literally melt. He was also gorgeous, which helped. I think you're a little bit more shallow when you're younger and talent tended to mean more to me than personality. Whereas now my wish list is topped by a good sense of humour.

What lengths would I go to, in order to attract a man I really fancied? Whatever it took, really! A girl's got to do what a girl's got to do. I'd still have to be me, though, and I couldn't pretend I liked something if I didn't. You know, if I met a bloke who liked drinking red wine I couldn't pretend to like it too. I have seen girls do that and I'm always like, 'No, don't do it!' If you're not being yourself it'll never last and, in my experience, it never does. We've all done things a bit out of the ordinary in the pursuit of love, but when you're in danger of losing your identity for the sake of attracting somebody you can't possibly keep it up.

With me, it's all or nothing and, as well as being myself, I'll always wear my heart on my sleeve and give it everything. I won't be like a psycho-stalker-bitch, but you know what I mean. Actually, I have been a bit stalker-ish sometimes. Not to the extent where the other party will take out an injunction or I'll boil one of their pets, but if I really like somebody and they don't reciprocate I won't give up straight away. It does get to a point, though, where I'll become pissed off and when that happens I'm done and, once I'm done, that really is it. Even if they came back and said they were interested, if I've gone into pissed-off mode they'll be dead to me. I'm over you now. Fuck off!

A few weeks ago somebody said, 'Saucy undies, yes or no?' Well, when I'm with someone, it's 'Yes,' but when I'm not, I'm in full-on Bridget Jones pants. In fact, now I'm back on the dating scene I'll have to get some new saucy undies – if a man saw me in what I wear at the moment, he'd never come back!

I have been known to dress up in the past and not just in saucy undies. I'm not talking first dates here, but when I've been with somebody for a while – you know, three or four days – they might get the sexy nurse's outfit. I'm sorry if that's put you off your tea; I'm only being honest! The thing is, dressing up only ever works for me if I'm the one doing it: if the person I'm with tries it too, it'll usually end in laughter. Put it this way – I once had to say to my other half (I'm not saying which one), 'I'm sorry, but I am not shagging you while you're dressed as Zorro!' He had worn the outfit with the intention of turning me on but, unfortunately, the sight turned me into a giggling wreck. 'First of all, you are not Antonio Banderas,' I said. 'And, secondly, I just can't!' I tell you what, had that other half actually been Antonio Banderas, he'd still be tied to the bed!

Even when I've put outfits on in the past I've done so kind of tongue-in-cheek and, even in the throes of passion, I've had to stop myself from laughing. It's so hard though. If somebody's really turned on by what you're wearing and all you want to do is start giggling, it's a disaster waiting to happen.

Like it or not, what you wear – whether it be a nurse's costume or an evening dress – kind of depends on what shape and age you are and, I dare say, in a few years' time I'll be swapping my nurse's outfit for a matron's! With some people, though, age doesn't come into it. Look at Jennifer Lopez, for instance. She's fifty-one and can wear anything a twenty-year-old would wear and she'll look fantastic. The rest of us have to take more notice of age and shape. If I went out wearing a mini-skirt and a tight top these days – as well as having a bloody good laugh at myself – I'd probably be arrested! I'd be like, 'Oh, my God, you look like mutton dressed as mutton!'

I don't mean to say that, at a certain age or with a particular shape, you can't dress alluringly any longer. You just have to wear something that complements your figure. I think being sexy should be left more to the imagination when you get to my age. Let's face it, it has to be! You know what I mean, though? Some of the sexiest people I've seen – men and women – wear normal clothes and aren't even trying (which is what makes them sexy!). When a person is wearing a pair of shorts and half their arse is showing, I'll think, No it's too obvious. For God's sake put it away!

That's what I mean about getting older. Some younger men like older women because of their age and experience. It fires their imaginations. I think it also has something to do with class, as in looking classy. I'm not saying everyone has it, but some women ooze class and that comes with age. Look at me, I'm dripping with fucking class, I am! Can't you tell?

So, tips for aspiring sex goddesses: well, apart from not shagging Zorro impersonators who aren't Antonio Banderas, I'd say go classy, especially if you're my age. It's far sexier than the tits-out approach although, if you're younger, that might work too. In fact, why not try both? A bit of cleavage is OK, but let them know what they *could* be winning at the end of the night.

Once you're in a relationship, well, it's down to whatever you're into, really! As long as it's legal. If you want to wear a PVC dominatrix outfit (and are confident that you'll be able to get out of it at the end of the evening without having to call for the fire brigade), go for your life! It's all about pleasing each other and if that floats your boat, why not?

That's something I could never do, though; become a dominatrix. I have thought about opening a brothel and becoming a madam but the problem is that, any time somebody asked me to spank them, I'd wet myself laughing. What I need are lots of very rich men who get turned on by women who spank them and then laugh at them at the same time. If you know any, get in touch.

Goddess of goddesses

This one is an all-round goddess really, just generally being fantastic. Once again, you'll have to use your imagination, given whose name is on the cover of this book, but thinking of what I put you through in the previous section this shouldn't be an issue!

Live. Laugh. Love.

I'll tell you what, let's start off with some philosophy on life, shall we? In all seriousness, I'd simply say be kind and don't judge people or think badly of them because they don't think like you. Let people be who they want to be, is basically what I'm saying. You can bitch about them when you're with your mates, of course, but to their face be kind!

My second philosophy of life comes from considering the point of view of the people I've just been talking about; basically, if you don't like who I am, fuck you! I would say that you should not change for anybody, regardless of what you think you might get out of doing so. I've talked a lot in this book about self-esteem and the world's greatest bitches-of-goddesses have bucketloads of it, and they have bucketloads because they're always true to themselves and refuse to compromise.

It took me donkey's years to occupy a similar situation and, although I would never describe myself as a goddess (although you might!), having the confidence to be who I really am is by far the best gift I've ever given myself. The message I'd give to anyone who doesn't like this would be – all together now – 'Fuck you!'

Just remember that you always have been and always will be a work-in-progress and there will be days when you wake up feeling depressed, ugly or fragile. What I had to do in order to improve in this department was train myself to both like and accept me, whatever was going on. Because I look after myself in this way, I'm able to try my best to be a good person. I don't always get it right, of course, and my thoughts don't always follow what I want to do, but my actions pull me through. Remember, just because your mind says that something or someone is a certain way, doesn't mean it is or they are.

One thing that might help you improve your self-esteem is forcing yourself to become more familiar with the positive aspects of your character and personality. If you're reading this book, for instance, you're obviously highly intelligent and you literally crap good taste, so there's two things, for a start! Seriously, though, the next time you look in the mirror and all you see and hear are negatives, just try focusing on what you like about yourself, both physically and emotionally.

You could choose your eyes, your hair or the fact that you're caring. You might have to do a bit of searching, especially if you've always been quite negative about yourself. Those elements are there, though, believe me, and you need to do that every day – not just once in a while. My self-esteem used to be almost non-existent and has only really become established over the last few years. I'm not a flaming big-head or anything, I just value myself now and know that I'm a person with faults who is always trying to be better. Remind yourself every day that, despite not being perfect, you will always be enough!

I live in a world where you're for ever having to think about pleasing other people, whether that be visually or verbally. I think I've battled with it all of my life, to be honest, and the realisation that it's all a load of bollocks and that I shouldn't give a shit what people think, within reason, is ultimately what set me free. There's no better feeling than knowing that you're authentically you. Trust me.

The thing is, though, regardless of how authentic you think you're being, if you're not surrounded by people of a similar mindset, remaining so is always going to be difficult. I'm not suggesting that you make any drastic changes, but if you don't have people in your life who are prepared to say to you, 'Look, Mother. You can't wear a nurse's outfit to cook tea in. You look ridiculous!' or, 'My God, you look gorgeous in that dress,' then you might need to think about the company you're keeping. The people closest to me – friends and family – are all prepared to call me out when I'm being an arsehole and big me up when I'm being a saint and, because they're my constant and are the people who matter to me, I'm able to go on working in what is really a very shallow industry.

Can I tell you when I finally stopped putting everyone else and everyone else's opinion before my own? I was doing a show on Channel 5 called *In Therapy* back in 2017, in which some sessions I had were recorded and analysed. I'd obviously had therapy before, but the woman they paired me with was very forceful and I even remember rowing with her at one point. I forget what she said now but it was in response to me and I remember thinking, No, you dickhead. You don't know me!

Apart from that, it all went really well until the end of the last session, when she suddenly said, 'But are you happy, Coleen?'

I think I'd been giving her a load of excuses for doing certain things, basically along the lines of, 'Well the kids are happy, so that's OK,' or, 'As long as they're happy then I'm happy,' etc. Then, when she finally asked if I was happy, I started to sob. It came totally out of the blue but it hit me like a train and I cried buckets.

Until that point, no one had ever asked if I was happy, and what made me cry was realising that I was anything but. I was fifty-two years old and had never been asked, or had asked myself, if I was happy. What's more, nobody seemed to care either way and the reason they didn't ask me is because they were happy.

Just to expand on this for a second, something else you really need to think about if you're going to consider coming over to this side and being a bitch of a goddess like *moi*, is being kind to yourself physically. The way you do that is by making time for yourself, maxing out your hubby's credit cards and finding yourself several toy boys. OK, so the second and third are optional, but the first one isn't.

There's a big self-care trend at the moment and it's not before time. Once again, though, this is something I've only come to very recently and includes things like my aforementioned eating habits, which I've recently changed, and just doing what I want to do occasionally. You have to have a balance, especially if you're single, and not confuse doing something nice or good for yourself with sitting on your arse all day or eating your own body weight in ice-cream. It was that kind of behaviour that led me to alter what I eat and, although I still treat myself, I can only do that if I'm doing something to balance it out. I'm sorry, girls, but when you get to our age, there really is no such thing as a free lunch!

Something else that's going to put you within touching distance of being a bitch of a goddess is taking risks and challenging yourself. Because of who manages me, I have no choice but to take challenges now and then and one of the biggest ones was doing *Dancing On Ice*. I said, 'No' at first but she said, 'I've told them you're doing it so, tough!'

Melanie knew I wouldn't find it easy but she also knew I had it in me to do it and I did. Don't get me wrong, I was shit, but I still did it! Another thing she made me do was a four-hundred-kilometre bike ride down the Nile. I did that without even training, although no amount of training could have prepared me for having such a sore arse!

When I completed the ride I had loads of people asking if I was going to do it again and I was like, 'No, I bloody well am not!' I do fancy challenging myself, though; if it's in aid of a good cause, then I'll give it a go. I can be talked into anything if you get me at the right moment! It's like people who climb Everest. I always think, Why would you want to do that, unless there was a Costa Coffee on top? It's not even getting up that would worry me, it would be getting down again.

As I've already said, I've never really been ambitious and that means I need other people to be ambitious for me! I do see programmes on telly sometimes and think, I'd like to have a go at that, but actually doing it is a different matter. That's the advice, then, if you want to be persuaded to go out of your comfort zone: find yourself a cheerleader who will always push you. Mine is my manager Melanie but yours might be your best friend or your partner. Melanie is a psychopath who pushes me to put on skates and make a tit of myself in front of millions of people. She's definitely my ambition but I think I'm hers, to a certain extent.

She was the one who talked me into having a go at acting. I was adamant I wouldn't be able to do it, but she said I would. How much of it was down to luck, I have no idea, but I'm glad she did it. I always end up shocking myself in these situations and, if you haven't done the same lately, you should think about giving it a go. You don't have to ride a bike four hundred kilometres down the Nile or go on *Dancing On Ice*. Leave that to idiots like me! Just remember, though, that – providing you give yourself a chance – you can do pretty much anything. Well, not *anything*, but you know what I mean. Just back yourself occasionally and do not let the bastards grind you down!

Well, that's just about it for now. This is the first time I've ever done a book like this and I genuinely hope it won't be the last. I do hope you've had a laugh, though. That's the one thing in life, apart from cigarettes, tea, dogs, cats and pygmy goats – and my kids, I suppose – that I genuinely don't think I could do without.

Live. Laugh. Love.

Thank God for me, though, because I've given myself more reasons to laugh over the years, just by making mistakes and being an idiot, than I care to remember!

Don't forget that you and me are – and will always be – a work-in-progress and, if you get it wrong occasionally or make a tit of yourself – like I do at least once a day – learn from it, laugh about it and, most importantly, enjoy the journey.

Bye for now X

Acknowledgements

To Andreas Campomar and his wonderful team at Constable for giving me the opportunity to do this book, and James Hogg for letting me write it so freely, allowing me to be totally me (swear words included).

To Amanda Beckman for always keeping me on track and working tirelessly in the background for so many years without complaint – thank you!

To my amazing brothers and sisters – for all we've experienced in our lives, good or bad, yet never losing the love we have for each other. I'm in awe of all of you, especially Anne and Linda, two of the strongest women I know. I love you all so much!

To my agent and manager, but more importantly friend, Melanie Blake. Thank you for ALWAYS believing in me and for constantly pushing me to believe in myself. I couldn't have got to this point without you. Over sixteen years together now . . . Wow, longer then both my marriages! Here's to many more.

Finally, my children Shane, Jake and Ciara, without whom I'd be nothing. I could actually write a whole book on how much I love you, how you inspire me every day and how you've helped me learn and grow into the woman I am today. No matter what happens in my life, as long as I have you three, I will have all I need!

I'd like to dedicate this book to you, the reader, for the support, loyalty and love that you continue to show me after all these years. You will never know how much it means to me.

Who knows what the next chapter in life will hold for any of us but, whatever it may be, always remember to live, laugh and love!

Coleen X